MznLnx

Missing Links Exam Preps

Exam Prep for

Introduction To Linear Algebra

Strang, 3rd Edition

The MznLnx Exam Prep is your link from the texbook and lecture to your exams.
The MznLnx Exam Preps are unauthorized and comprehensive reviews of your textbooks.

All material provided by MznLnx and Rico Publications (c) 2010
Textbook publishers and textbook authors do not particpate in or contribute to these reviews.

MznLnx

Rico
Publications

Exam Prep for Introduction To Linear Algebra
3rd Edition
Strang

Publisher: Raymond Houge
Assistant Editor: Michael Rouger
Text and Cover Designer: Lisa Buckner
Marketing Manager: Sara Swagger
Project Manager, Editorial Production: Jerry Emerson
Art Director: Vernon Lowerui

Product Manager: Dave Mason
Editorial Assitant: Rachel Guzmanji
Pedagogy: Debra Long
Cover Image: Jim Reed/Getty Images
Text and Cover Printer: City Printing, Inc.
Compositor: Media Mix, Inc.

(c) 2010 Rico Publications
ALL RIGHTS RESERVED. No part of this work covered by the copyright may be reproduced or used in any form or by any means--graphic, electronic, or mechanical, including photocopying, recording, taping, Web distribution, information storage, and retrieval systems, or in any other manner--without the written permission of the publisher.

For more information about our products, contact us at:
Dave.Mason@RicoPublications.com

For permission to use material from this text or product, submit a request online to:
Dave.Mason@RicoPublications.com

Printed in the United States
ISBN:

Contents

CHAPTER 1
Introduction to Vectors — 1
CHAPTER 2
Solving Linear Equations — 9
CHAPTER 3
Vector Spaces and Subspaces — 29
CHAPTER 4
Orthogonality — 36
CHAPTER 5
Determinants — 44
CHAPTER 6
Eigenvalues and Eigenvectors — 56
CHAPTER 7
Linear Transformations — 76
CHAPTER 8
Applications — 87
CHAPTER 9
Numerical Linear Algebra — 96
CHAPTER 10
Complex Vectors and Matrices — 106
ANSWER KEY — 115

TO THE STUDENT

COMPREHENSIVE

The *MznLnx* Exam Prep series is designed to help you pass your exams. Editors at MznLnx review your textbooks and then prepare these practice exams to help you master the textbook material. Unlike study guides, workbooks, and practice tests provided by the texbook publisher and textbook authors, *MznLnx* gives you **all** of the material in each chapter in exam form, not just samples, so you can be sure to nail your exam.

MECHANICAL

The MznLnx Exam Prep series creates exams that will help you learn the subject matter as well as test you on your understanding. Each question is designed to help you master the concept. Just working through the exams, you gain an understanding of the subject--its a simple mechanical process that produces success.

INTEGRATED STUDY GUIDE AND REVIEW

MznLnx is not just a set of exams designed to test you, its also a comprehensive review of the subject content. Each exam question is also a review of the concept, making sure that you will get the answer correct without having to go to other sources of material. You learn as you go! Its the easiest way to pass an exam.

HUMOR

Studying can be tedious and dry. MznLnx's instructional design includes moderate humor within the exam questions on occassion, to break the tedium and revitalize the brain

Chapter 1. Introduction to Vectors

1. In mathematics, in the field of group theory, a _____ of a finite group is a quasisimple subnormal subgroup. Any two distinct components commute. The product of all the components is the layer of the group.
   a. Group homomorphism
   b. Wreath product
   c. Stallings' theorem about ends of groups
   d. Component

2. In mathematics, _____ are a concept central to linear algebra and related fields of mathematics

   Suppose that K is a field and V is a vector space over K. As usual, we call elements of V vectors and call elements of K scalars.

   a. Hyperstructures
   b. Left alternative
   c. Groupoid
   d. Linear combinations

3. In mathematics, a _____ of a number x is any number which, when repeatedly multiplied by itself, eventually yields x:

   $$r \times r \times \cdots \times r = x.$$

   In terms of exponentiation, r is a _____ of x if

   $$r^n = x$$

   for some positive integer n. For example, 2 is a _____ of 16 since $2^4 = 2 \times 2 \times 2 \times 2 = 16$.

   The number n is called the degree of the _____.

   a. Difference of two squares
   b. Root
   c. Rationalisation
   d. Cubic function

4. In mathematics, particularly linear algebra, a _____ is a matrix with all its entries being zero. Some examples of zero matrices are

   $$0_{1,1} = \begin{bmatrix} 0 \end{bmatrix}, \ 0_{2,2} = \begin{bmatrix} 0 & 0 \\ 0 & 0 \end{bmatrix}, \ 0_{2,3} = \begin{bmatrix} 0 & 0 & 0 \\ 0 & 0 & 0 \end{bmatrix},$$

   The set of m×n matrices with entries in a ring K forms a ring $K_{m,n}$. The _____ $0_{K_{m,n}}$ in $K_{m,n}$ is the matrix with all entries equal to 0_K, where 0_K is the additive identity in K.

   a. Complex Hadamard matrix
   b. Zero matrix
   c. Regular Hadamard matrix
   d. Normal matrix

5. In mathematics, a _____ is a rectangular array of numbers. This way, matrices can record data that depend on multiple parameters. In particular they are used to keep track of the coefficients of multiple linear equations. Matrices are closely connected to linear transformations, which are higher-dimensional analogs of linear functions, i.e., functions of the form f(x) = c Â· x, where c is a constant. This map corresponds to a _____ with one row and column, with entry c. In addition to a number of elementary, entrywise operations such as _____ addition a key notion is _____ multiplication, which displays a number of features not encountered in numbers; for example, products of matrices depend on the order of the factors, unlike products of real numbers, say, where c Â· d = d Â· c for any two numbers c and d.

a. Matrix
b. Commutativity
c. Polynomial expression
d. Heap

6. The real component of a quaternion is also called its _____ part.

The term is also sometimes used informally to mean a vector, matrix, tensor, or other usually 'compound' value that is actually reduced to a single component. Thus, for example, the product of a 1×n matrix and an n×1 matrix, which is formally a 1×1 matrix, is often said to be a _____.

a. Scalar
b. Self-adjoint
c. Tensor product
d. Distributivity

7. In mathematics, _____ is one of the basic operations defining a vector space in linear algebra Note that _____ is different from scalar product which is an inner product between two vectors.

More specifically, if K is a field and V is a vector space over K, then _____ is a function from K × V to V. The result of applying this function to c in K and v in V is denoted cv.

a. Matrix pencil
b. Symplectic vector space
c. K-frame
d. Scalar multiplication

8. _____ is the mathematical process of putting things together. The plus sign '+' means that numbers are added together. For example, in the picture on the right, there are 3 + 2 apples--meaning three apples and two other apples--which is the same as five apples, since 3 + 2 = 5.

a. Abelian P-root group
b. AKS primality test
c. ADE classification
d. Addition

9. An _____ is a pointed projectile that is shot with a bow. It predates recorded history and is common to most cultures. Schematic of an _____ with many parts.

A normal _____ consists of a shaft with an arrowhead attached to the front end, with fletchings and a nock at the other.

a. ADE classification
b. Abelian P-root group
c. Arrow
d. AKS primality test

10. In geometry, a _____ is a quadrilateral with two sets of parallel sides. The opposite or facing sides of a _____ are of equal length, and the opposite angles of a _____ are of equal size. The three-dimensional counterpart of a _____ is a parallelepiped.

a. -equivalence
b. -module
c. 2-bridge knot
d. Parallelogram

11. In linear algebra, a _____ or column matrix is an m × 1 matrix, i.e. a matrix consisting of a single column of m elements.

$$\mathbf{x} = \begin{bmatrix} x_1 \\ x_2 \\ \vdots \\ x_m \end{bmatrix}$$

The transpose of a _____ is a row vector and vice versa.

The set of all column vectors forms a vector space which is the dual space to the set of all row vectors.

a. K-frame
b. Normal basis
c. Symplectic vector space
d. Column vector

12. In mathematics and statistics, a _____ or stochastic vector is a vector with non-negative entries that add up to one.

The positions (indices) of a _____ represent the possible outcomes of a discrete random variable, and the vector gives us the probability mass function of that random variable, which is the standard way of characterizing a discrete probability distribution.

Here are some examples of probability vectors:

$$x_0 = \begin{bmatrix} 0.5 \\ 0.25 \\ 0.25 \end{bmatrix}, \quad x_1 = \begin{bmatrix} 0 \\ 1 \\ 0 \end{bmatrix}, \quad x_2 = \begin{bmatrix} 0.65 \\ 0.35 \end{bmatrix}, \quad x_3 = \begin{bmatrix} 0.3 \\ 0.5 \\ 0.07 \\ 0.1 \\ 0.03 \end{bmatrix}.$$

Writing out the vector components of a vector p as

$$p = \begin{bmatrix} p_1 \\ p_2 \\ \vdots \\ p_n \end{bmatrix}$$

the vector components must sum to one:

$$\sum_{i=1}^{n} p_i = 1$$

One also has the requirement that each individual component must have a probability between zero and one:

$$0 \leq p_i \leq 1$$

for all i.

a. Probability vector
b. -module
c. 2-bridge knot
d. -equivalence

13. If the space is two-dimensional, then a half-space is called a _____ A half-space in a one-dimensional space is called a ray.

A half-space may be specified by a linear inequality, derived from the linear equation that specifies the defining hyperplane.

a. 2-bridge knot
b. Half-plane
c. -equivalence
d. -module

14. A _____ is a three-dimensional solid object bounded by six square faces, facets or sides, with three meeting at each vertex. The _____ can also be called a regular hexahedron and is one of the five Platonic solids. It is a special kind of square prism, of rectangular parallelepiped and of trigonal trapezohedron.

a. 2-bridge knot
b. Cube
c. -equivalence
d. -module

15. In mathematics, the _____ is an operation which takes two vectors over the real numbers R and returns a real-valued scalar quantity. It is the standard inner product of the orthonormal Euclidean space. It contrasts with the cross product which produces a vector result.

a. Complex structure
b. Coefficient matrix
c. Dot product
d. Centrosymmetric matrix

16. In abstract algebra, the _____ of a module is a measure of the module's 'size'. It is defined as the _____ of the longest ascending chain of submodules and is a generalization of the concept of dimension for vector spaces. The modules with finite _____ share many important properties with finite-dimensional vector spaces.

a. Finitely generated module
b. Supermodule
c. Length
d. Morita equivalence

17. In linear algebra, functional analysis and related areas of mathematics, a _____ is a function that assigns a strictly positive length or size to all vectors in a vector space, other than the zero vector. A seminorm (or pseudonorm), on the other hand, is allowed to assign zero length to some non-zero vectors.

A simple example is the 2-dimensional Euclidean space R^2 equipped with the Euclidean _____.

a. -equivalence
b. Norm
c. -module
d. Quasinorm

18. In mathematics, a _____ in a (unital) ring R is an invertible element of R, i.e. an element u such that there is a v in R with

$$uv = vu = 1_R,$$ where 1_R is the multiplicative identity element.

That is, u is an invertible element of the multiplicative monoid of R. If $0 \neq 1$ in the ring, then 0 is not a _____.

Unfortunately, the term _____ is also used to refer to the identity element 1_R of the ring, in expressions like ring with a _____ or _____ ring, and also e.g. '_____' matrix.

  a. Ascending chain condition on principal ideals
  b. Unit
  c. Ore extension
  d. Ore condition

19. In mathematics, two vectors are _____ if they are perpendicular, i.e., they form a right angle. The word comes from the Greek á½€pθίŒς , meaning 'straight', and γωνῖα (gonia), meaning 'angle'. For example, a subway and the street above, although they do not physically intersect, are _____ if they cross at a right angle.
  a. Orthogonal
  b. Unital
  c. Embedding
  d. Expression

20. In geometry, two lines or planes (or a line and a plane), are considered _____ to each other if they form congruent adjacent angles (an L-shape.) The term may be used as a noun or adjective. Thus, referring to Figure 1, the line AB is the _____ to CD through the point B. Note that by definition, a line is infinitely long, and strictly speaking AB and CD in this example represent line segments of two infinitely long lines.
  a. -module
  b. -equivalence
  c. 2-bridge knot
  d. Perpendicular

21. The _____ of an angle is the ratio of the length of the adjacent side to the length of the hypotenuse. In our case

$$\cos A = \frac{\text{adjacent}}{\text{hypotenuse}} = \frac{b}{h}.$$

The tangent of an angle is the ratio of the length of the opposite side to the length of the adjacent side. In our case

$$\tan A = \frac{\text{opposite}}{\text{adjacent}} = \frac{a}{b}.$$

The remaining three functions are best defined using the above three functions.

  a. 2-bridge knot
  b. -module
  c. -equivalence
  d. Cosine

22. In geometry and trigonometry, an _____ is the figure formed by two rays sharing a common endpoint, called the vertex of the _____ . The magnitude of the _____ is the 'amount of rotation' that separates the two rays, and can be measured by considering the length of circular arc swept out when one ray is rotated about the vertex to coincide with the other Where there is no possibility of confusion, the term '_____' is used interchangeably for both the geometric configuration itself and for its angular magnitude (which is simply a numerical quantity).

a. Abelian P-root group
c. ADE classification
b. AKS primality test
d. Angle

23. The _____, in mathematics, is a type of mean or average, which indicates the central tendency or typical value of a set of numbers. It is similar to the arithmetic mean, which is what most people think of with the word 'average,' except that instead of adding the set of numbers and then dividing the sum by the count of numbers in the set, n, the numbers are multiplied and then the nth root of the resulting product is taken.

For instance, the _____ of two numbers, say 2 and 8, is just the square root (i.e., the second root) of their product, 16, which is 4.

a. -module
c. Geometric mean
b. 2-bridge knot
d. -equivalence

24. In mathematics, the Cauchy-_____ the Cauchy inequality is a useful inequality encountered in many different settings, such as linear algebra applied to vectors, in analysis applied to infinite series and integration of products, and in probability theory, applied to variances and covariances. The general formulation of the Heisenberg uncertainty principle is derived using the Cauchy-_____ in the Hilbert space of pure quantum states.

The inequality for sums was published by , while the corresponding inequality for integrals was first stated by and rediscovered by

a. Schwarz inequality
c. -equivalence
b. -module
d. 2-bridge knot

25. In mathematics, an _____ is a statement about the relative size or order of two objects, or about whether they are the same or not

- The notation a < b means that a is less than b.
- The notation a > b means that a is greater than b.
- The notation a ≠ b means that a is not equal to b, but does not say that one is bigger than the other or even that they can be compared in size.

In all these cases, a is not equal to b, hence, '_____'.

These relations are known as strict _____

- The notation a ≤ b means that a is less than or equal to b (or, equivalently, not greater than b);
- The notation a ≥ b means that a is greater than or equal to b (or, equivalently, not smaller than b);

An additional use of the notation is to show that one quantity is much greater than another, normally by several orders of magnitude.

- The notation a ≪ b means that a is much less than b.
- The notation a ≫ b means that a is much greater than b.

If the sense of the _____ is the same for all values of the variables for which its members are defined, then the _____ is called an 'absolute' or 'unconditional' _____. If the sense of an _____ holds only for certain values of the variables involved, but is reversed or destroyed for other values of the variables, it is called a conditional _____.

One can apply the same algebraic operations to inequalities as one would apply for solving equalities. For example, to find x for the _____ 10x > 20 one would divide 20 by 10 to obtain x > 2.

a. AKS primality test
c. ADE classification
b. Abelian P-root group
d. Inequality

26. A _____ is one of the basic shapes of geometry: a polygon with three corners or vertices and three sides or edges which are line segments. A _____ with vertices A, B, and C is denoted ABC.

In Euclidean geometry any three non-collinear points determine a unique _____ and a unique plane (i.e. a two-dimensional Euclidean space.)

a. -module
c. 2-bridge knot
b. -equivalence
d. Triangle

27. In mathematics, the _____ states that for any triangle, the length of a given side must be less than the sum of the other two sides but greater than the difference between the two sides.

In Euclidean geometry and some other geometries this is a theorem. In the Euclidean case, in both the less than or equal to and greater than or equal to statements, equality occurs only if the triangle has a 180° angle and two 0° angles, as shown in the bottom example in the image to the right.

a. -equivalence
c. 2-bridge knot
b. -module
d. Triangle inequality

28. In trigonometry, the _____ is a statement about a general triangle which relates the lengths of its sides to the cosine of one of its angles. Using notation as in Fig. 1, the _____ states that

$$c^2 = a^2 + b^2 - 2ab\cos(\gamma),$$

or, equivalently:

$$b^2 = c^2 + a^2 - 2ca\cos(\beta),$$

$$a^2 = b^2 + c^2 - 2bc\cos(\alpha),$$

$$\cos(\gamma) = \frac{a^2 + b^2 - c^2}{2ab},$$

$$\cos(\beta) = \frac{a^2 + c^2 - b^2}{2ca},$$

$$\cos(\alpha) = \frac{b^2 + c^2 - a^2}{2bc}.$$

Note that c is the side opposite of angle γ, and that a and b are the two sides enclosing γ.

a. -module
b. 2-bridge knot
c. Law of cosines
d. -equivalence

29. A _____ is a triangle in which one angle is a right angle.

The side opposite the right angle is called the hypotenuse (side [BC] in the figure below.) In addition, the sides adjacent to the right angle are called legs or catheti (singular: cathetus.)

a. Right triangle
b. -module
c. -equivalence
d. 2-bridge knot

Chapter 2. Solving Linear Equations

1. In mathematics, a _____ is a bijection between skew diagrams satisfying certain properties, introduced by Zelevinsky (1981) in a generalization of the Robinson-Schensted correspondence and the Littlewood-Richardson rule.

   a. Macdonald polynomials
   b. -module
   c. Picture
   d. -equivalence

2. In mathematics, a _____ is a constant multiplicative factor of a certain object. For example, in the expression $9x^2$, the _____ of x^2 is 9.

   The object can be such things as a variable, a vector, a function, etc.

   a. Constant term
   b. Vandermonde polynomial
   c. Tschirnhaus transformation
   d. Coefficient

3. In linear algebra, the _____ refers to a matrix consisting of the coefficients of the variables in a set of linear equations.

   In general, a system with m linear equations and n unknowns can be written as

   $$a_{11}x_1 + a_{12}x_2 + ... + a_{1n}x_n = b_1$$
   $$a_{21}x_1 + a_{22}x_2 + ... + a_{2n}x_n = b_2$$
   $$\vdots$$
   $$a_{m1}x_1 + a_{m2}x_2 + ... + a_{mn}x_n = b_m$$

   where $x_1, x_2, ..., x_n$ are the unknowns and the numbers $a_{11}, a_{12}, ..., a_{mn}$ are the coefficients of the system. The _____ is the mxn matrix with the coefficient a_{ij} as the (i,j)-th entry:

   $$\begin{bmatrix} a_{11} & a_{12} & \cdots & a_{1n} \\ a_{21} & a_{22} & \cdots & a_{2n} \\ \vdots & \vdots & \ddots & \vdots \\ a_{m1} & a_{m2} & \cdots & a_{mn} \end{bmatrix}$$

   a. Centrosymmetric matrix
   b. Segre classification
   c. Coefficient matrix
   d. Linear inequality

4. In mathematics, _____ are a concept central to linear algebra and related fields of mathematics

   Suppose that K is a field and V is a vector space over K. As usual, we call elements of V vectors and call elements of K scalars.

   a. Hyperstructures
   b. Groupoid
   c. Left alternative
   d. Linear combinations

Chapter 2. Solving Linear Equations

5. In mathematics, a _____ is a rectangular array of numbers. This way, matrices can record data that depend on multiple parameters. In particular they are used to keep track of the coefficients of multiple linear equations. Matrices are closely connected to linear transformations, which are higher-dimensional analogs of linear functions, i.e., functions of the form f(x) = c Â· x, where c is a constant. This map corresponds to a _____ with one row and column, with entry c. In addition to a number of elementary, entrywise operations such as _____ addition a key notion is _____ multiplication, which displays a number of features not encountered in numbers; for example, products of matrices depend on the order of the factors, unlike products of real numbers, say, where c Â· d = d Â· c for any two numbers c and d.

   a. Polynomial expression
   b. Heap
   c. Commutativity
   d. Matrix

6. In linear algebra, the _____ or unit matrix of size n is the n-by-n square matrix with ones on the main diagonal and zeros elsewhere. It is denoted by I_n, or simply by I if the size is immaterial or can be trivially determined by the context. (In some fields, such as quantum mechanics, the _____ is denoted by a boldface one, 1; otherwise it is identical to I.)

   a. Associativity
   b. Orthogonal
   c. Identity matrix
   d. Artinian ideal

7. In mathematics, an element x of a ring R is called _____ if there exists some positive integer n such that $x^n = 0$.

   The term was introduced by Benjamin Peirce in the context of elements of an algebra that vanish when raised to a power.

   - This definition can be applied in particular to square matrices. The matrix

   $$A = \begin{pmatrix} 0 & 1 & 0 \\ 0 & 0 & 1 \\ 0 & 0 & 0 \end{pmatrix}$$

   is _____ because $A^3 = 0$. See _____ matrix for more.

   a. Nilpotent
   b. Product ring
   c. Ring of integers
   d. Hochschild homology

8. In linear algebra, a _____ is a square matrix N such that

   $$N^k = 0$$

   for some positive integer k. The smallest such k is sometimes called the degree of N.

   More generally, a nilpotent transformation is a linear transformation L of a vector space such that $L^k = 0$ for some positive integer k.

   a. Nilpotent matrix
   b. Shift matrix
   c. Pascal matrix
   d. Main diagonal

Chapter 2. Solving Linear Equations

9. The _____ of an angle is the ratio of the length of the adjacent side to the length of the hypotenuse. In our case

$$\cos A = \frac{\text{adjacent}}{\text{hypotenuse}} = \frac{b}{h}.$$

The tangent of an angle is the ratio of the length of the opposite side to the length of the adjacent side. In our case

$$\tan A = \frac{\text{opposite}}{\text{adjacent}} = \frac{a}{b}.$$

The remaining three functions are best defined using the above three functions.

- a. 2-bridge knot
- b. -equivalence
- c. -module
- d. Cosine

10. A matrix equation in the form $\mathbf{Lx = b}$ or $\mathbf{Ux = b}$ is very easy to solve by an iterative process called forward substitution for lower triangular matrices and analogously _____ for upper triangular matrices. The process is so called because for lower triangular matrices, one first computes x_1, then substitutes that forward into the next equation to solve for x_2, and repeats through to x_n. In an upper triangular matrix, one works backwards, first computing x_n, then substituting that back into the previous equation to solve for x_{n-1}, and repeating through x_1.

- a. -equivalence
- b. Back substitution
- c. 2-bridge knot
- d. -module

11. _____ is called _____ matrix or right triangular matrix.

The standard operations on triangular matrices conveniently preserve the triangular form: the sum and product of two _____ matrices is again _____. The inverse of an _____ matrix is also _____, and of course we can multiply an _____ matrix by a constant and it will still be _____.

- a. Abelian P-root group
- b. ADE classification
- c. AKS primality test
- d. Upper triangular

12. _____ is called _____ or right triangular matrix.

The standard operations on triangular matrices conveniently preserve the triangular form: the sum and product of two upper triangular matrices is again upper triangular. The inverse of an _____ is also upper triangular, and of course we can multiply an _____ by a constant and it will still be upper triangular.

- a. Abelian P-root group
- b. AKS primality test
- c. Upper triangular matrix
- d. ADE classification

13. In the mathematical discipline of linear algebra, a _____ is a special kind of square matrix where the entries either below or above the main diagonal are zero. Because matrix equations with triangular matrices are easier to solve they are very important in numerical analysis. The LU decomposition gives an algorithm to decompose any invertible matrix A into a normed lower triangle matrix L and an upper triangle matrix U.

    a. Triangular matrix   b. Diagonally dominant
    c. Hilbert matrix   d. Circulant matrix

14. In mathematics, especially linear algebra, the _____ is a special case of a permutation matrix, where the 1 elements reside on the counterdiagonal and all other elements are zero. In other words, it is a 'row-reversed' or 'column-reversed' version of the identity matrix.

$$J_2 = \begin{pmatrix} 0 & 1 \\ 1 & 0 \end{pmatrix}; \quad J_3 = \begin{pmatrix} 0 & 0 & 1 \\ 0 & 1 & 0 \\ 1 & 0 & 0 \end{pmatrix}; \quad J_n = \begin{pmatrix} 0 & 0 & \cdots & 0 & 0 & 1 \\ 0 & 0 & \cdots & 0 & 1 & 0 \\ 0 & 0 & \cdots & 1 & 0 & 0 \\ \vdots & \vdots & & \vdots & \vdots & \vdots \\ 0 & 1 & \cdots & 0 & 0 & 0 \\ 1 & 0 & \cdots & 0 & 0 & 0 \end{pmatrix}.$$

If J is an n×n _____, then the elements of J are defined such that:

$$J_{i,j} = \begin{cases} 1, & j = n - i \\ 0, & j \neq n - i \end{cases}$$

- $J^T = J$.
- $J^n = I$ for even n; $J^n = J$ for odd n, where n is any integer. Thus J is an involutary matrix; that is, $J^{-1} = J$.
- The trace of J is 1 if n is odd, and 0 if n is even.

- Any matrix A satisfying the condition AJ = JA is said to be centrosymmetric.
- Any matrix A satisfying the condition AJ = JA^T is said to be persymmetric.

    a. Exchange matrix   b. Arithmetical
    c. Analytic subgroup   d. Ordered vector space

15. In linear algebra, _____ is an efficient algorithm for solving systems of linear equations, finding the rank of a matrix, and calculating the inverse of an invertible square matrix. _____ is named after German mathematician and scientist Carl Friedrich Gauss.

Elementary row operations are used to reduce a matrix to row echelon form.

    a. 2-bridge knot   b. -module
    c. -equivalence   d. Gaussian elimination

16. If $A_1, A_2, ..., A_n$ are _____ square matrices over a field, then

Chapter 2. Solving Linear Equations

$$(A_1 A_2 \cdots A_n)^{-1} = A_n^{-1} A_{n-1}^{-1} \cdots A_1^{-1}.$$

It becomes evident why this is the case if one attempts to find an inverse for the product of the A_is from first principles, that is, that we wish to determine B such that

$$(A_1 A_2 \cdots A_n) B = I$$

where B is the inverse matrix of the product. To remove A_1 from the product, we can then write

$$A_1^{-1}(A_1 A_2 \cdots A_n) B = A_1^{-1} I$$

which would reduce the equation to

$$(A_2 A_3 \cdots A_n) B = A_1^{-1} I.$$

Likewise, then, from

$$A_2^{-1}(A_2 A_3 \cdots A_n) B = A_2^{-1} A_1^{-1} I$$

which simplifies to

$$(A_3 A_4 \cdots A_n) B = A_2^{-1} A_1^{-1} I.$$

If one repeat the process up to A_n, the equation becomes

$$B = A_n^{-1} A_{n-1}^{-1} \cdots A_2^{-1} A_1^{-1} I$$

$$B = A_n^{-1} A_{n-1}^{-1} \cdots A_2^{-1} A_1^{-1}$$

but B is the inverse matrix, i.e. $B = (A_1 A_2 \cdots A_n)^{-1}$ so the property is established.

Over the field of real numbers, the set of singular n-by-n matrices, considered as a subset of $R^{n \times n}$, is a null set, i.e., has Lebesgue measure zero.

a. -module
c. 2-bridge knot
b. -equivalence
d. Nonsingular

17. In mathematics, the _____ is an operation which takes two vectors over the real numbers R and returns a real-valued scalar quantity. It is the standard inner product of the orthonormal Euclidean space. It contrasts with the cross product which produces a vector result.

   a. Coefficient matrix   b. Complex structure
   c. Dot product   d. Centrosymmetric matrix

18. In mathematics, especially in linear algebra and matrix theory, the duplication matrix and the _____ are linear transformations used for transforming half-vectorizations of matrices into vectorizations or (respectively) vice-versa.

The duplication matrix D_n is the unique $n^2 \times n(n+1)/2$ matrix which, for any $n \times n$ symmetric matrix A, transforms vech(A) into vec(A):

$$D_n \text{ vech}(A) = \text{vec}(A.)$$

For the 2×2 symmetric matrix $A = \begin{bmatrix} a & b \\ b & d \end{bmatrix}$, this transformation reads

$$\begin{bmatrix} 1 & 0 & 0 \\ 0 & 1 & 0 \\ 0 & 1 & 0 \\ 0 & 0 & 1 \end{bmatrix} \begin{bmatrix} a \\ b \\ d \end{bmatrix} = \begin{bmatrix} a \\ b \\ b \\ d \end{bmatrix}$$

The _____ L_n is the unique $n(n+1)/2 \times n^2$ matrix which, for any $n \times n$ matrix A, transforms vec(A) into vech(A):

$$L_n \text{ vec}(A) = \text{vech}(A.)$$

   a. ADE classification   b. AKS primality test
   c. Elimination matrix   d. Abelian P-root group

19. In mathematics, an _____ is a simple matrix which differs from the identity matrix in a minimal way. The elementary matrices generate the general linear group of invertible matrices, and left (respectively, right) multiplication by an _____ represent elementary row operations (respectively, elementary column operations.)

In algebraic K-theory, 'elementary matrices' refers only to the row-addition matrices.

   a. Orthogonalization   b. Orthonormal basis
   c. Orientation   d. Elementary matrix

20. Formally, a binary operation $*$ on a set S is called associative if it satisfies the _____:

$(x * y) * z = x * (y * z)$ for all $x, y, z \in S$.
Using * to denote a binary operation performed on a set

$(xy)z = x(yz) = xyz$ for all $x, y, z \in S$.
An example of multiplicative associativity

The evaluation order does not affect the value of such expressions, and it can be shown that the same holds for expressions containing any number of ∗ operations. Thus, when ∗ is associative, the evaluation order can therefore be left unspecified without causing ambiguity, by omitting the parentheses and writing simply:

xyz,

However, it is important to remember that changing the order of operations does not involve or permit changing the actual operations themselves by moving the operands around within the expression.

A very different perspective is obtained by rephrasing associativity using functional notation: f(f(x,y),z) = f(x,f(y,z)): when expressed in this form, associativity becomes less obvious.

a. ADE classification
c. Abelian P-root group

b. Associative law
d. AKS primality test

21. In several fields of mathematics the term _____ is used with different but closely related meanings. They all relate to the notion of mapping the elements of a set to other elements of the same set, i.e., exchanging (or 'permuting') elements of a set.

The general concept of _____ can be defined more formally in different contexts:

In combinatorics, a _____ is usually understood to be a sequence containing each element from a finite set once, and only once.

a. Near-field
c. Binary function

b. Permutation
d. Rupture field

22. In mathematics, in matrix theory, a _____ is a square (0,1)-matrix that has exactly one entry 1 in each row and each column and 0's elsewhere. Each such matrix represents a specific permutation of m elements and, when used to multiply another matrix, can produce that permutation in the rows or columns of the other matrix.

Given a permutation π of m elements,

$$\pi : \{1, \ldots, m\} \to \{1, \ldots, m\}$$

given in two-line form by

$$\begin{pmatrix} 1 & 2 & \cdots & m \\ \pi(1) & \pi(2) & \cdots & \pi(m) \end{pmatrix},$$

its _____ is the m × m matrix P_π whose entries are all 0 except that in row i, the entry π(i) equals 1.

a. Main diagonal
c. Skew-symmetric
b. Hessenberg matrix
d. Permutation matrix

23. In linear algebra, the _____ of a matrix is obtained by changing a matrix in some way.

Given the matrices A and B, where:

$$A = \begin{bmatrix} 1 & 3 & 2 \\ 2 & 0 & 1 \\ 5 & 2 & 2 \end{bmatrix}, \quad B = \begin{bmatrix} 4 \\ 3 \\ 1 \end{bmatrix}$$

Then, the _____ is written as:

$$(A|B) = \begin{bmatrix} 1 & 3 & 2 & 4 \\ 2 & 0 & 1 & 3 \\ 5 & 2 & 2 & 1 \end{bmatrix}$$

This is useful when solving systems of linear equations or the _____ may also be used to find the inverse of a matrix by combining it with the identity matrix.

$$C = \begin{bmatrix} 1 & 3 \\ -5 & 0 \end{bmatrix}$$

Let C be a square 2×2 matrix where

To find the inverse of C we create (C | I) where I is the 2×2 identity matrix.

a. Unistochastic matrix
c. Euclidean distance matrix
b. Unitary matrix
d. Augmented matrix

24. In mathematics, particularly matrix theory and combinatorics, the _____ is an infinite matrix containing the binomial coefficients as its elements. There are 3 ways this can be achieved - either as an upper-triangular matrix, a lower-triangular matrix, or as a symmetric matrix. The 5×5 truncations of these are shown below.

a. Polynomial matrix
c. Butson-type
b. Conference matrix
d. Pascal matrix

25. In mathematics, and in particular in abstract algebra, distributivity is a property of binary operations that generalises the _____ from elementary algebra. For example: <_____>
    $2 \times (1 + 3) = (2 \times 1) + (2 \times 3).$

In the left-hand side of the above equation, the 2 multiplies the sum of 1 and 3; on the right-hand side, it multiplies the 1 and the 3 individually, with the results added afterwards.

a. -module
c. Distributive law
b. 2-bridge knot
d. -equivalence

26. In mathematics and group theory, a _____ system for the action of a group G on a set X is a partition of X that is G-invariant. In terms of the associated equivalence relation on X, G-invariance means that

$x \equiv y$ implies $gx \equiv gy$

for all g in G and all x, y in X. The action of G on X determines a natural action of G on any _____ system for X.

Each element of the _____ system is called a _____.

a. Symmetric group
c. Parker vector
b. Block
d. Frobenius group

27. In the mathematical discipline of matrix theory, a _____ or a partitioned matrix is a partition of a matrix into rectangular smaller matrices called blocks. Looking at it another way, the matrix is written in terms of smaller matrices written side-by-side. A _____ must conform to a consistent way of splitting up the rows, and the columns: we group the rows into some adjacent 'bunches', and the columns likewise.

a. Symplectic matrix
c. Bidiagonal matrix
b. Block matrix
d. Vandermonde matrix

Chapter 2. Solving Linear Equations

28. In elementary algebra, a _____ is a polynomial with two terms--the sum of two monomials--often bound by parenthesis or brackets when operated upon. It is the simplest kind of polynomial other than monomials.

- The _____ $a^2 - b^2$ can be factored as the product of two other binomials:

$$a^2 - b^2 = (a + b)(a - b.)$$

This is a special case of the more general formula:

$$a^{n+1} - b^{n+1} = (a - b) \sum_{k=0}^{n} a^k b^{n-k}.$$

- The product of a pair of linear binomials (ax + b) and (cx + d) is:

$$(ax + b)(cx + d) = acx^2 + axd + bcx + bd.$$

- A _____ raised to the nth power, represented as

$$(a + b)^n$$

can be expanded by means of the _____ theorem or, equivalently, using Pascal's triangle. Taking a simple example, the perfect square _____ $(p + q)^2$ can be found by squaring the :first digit, adding twice the product of the first and second digit and finally adding the square of the second digit, to give $p^2 + 2pq + q^2$.

a. Theory of equations
b. Generalized arithmetic progression
c. Content
d. Binomial

29. A _____ is a three-dimensional solid object bounded by six square faces, facets or sides, with three meeting at each vertex. The _____ can also be called a regular hexahedron and is one of the five Platonic solids. It is a special kind of square prism, of rectangular parallelepiped and of trigonal trapezohedron.

a. -module
b. -equivalence
c. 2-bridge knot
d. Cube

30. In mathematics, the _____ of a vector space V is the cardinality (i.e. the number of vectors) of a basis of V. It is sometimes called Hamel _____ or algebraic _____ to distinguish it from other types of _____. All bases of a vector space have equal cardinality and so the _____ of a vector space is uniquely defined. The _____ of the vector space V over the field F can be written as $\dim_F(V)$ or as [V : F], read '_____ of V over F'.

a. Cofactor
b. Dimension
c. Dual basis
d. Partial trace

31. In geometry, a _____ is an n-dimensional analogue of a square (n = 2) and a cube (n = 3.) It is a closed, compact, convex figure whose 1-skeleton consists of groups of opposite parallel line segments aligned in each of the space's dimensions, at right angles to each other and of the same length.

An n-dimensional _____ is also called an n-cube.

a. -equivalence
b. -module
c. Hypercube
d. 2-bridge knot

Chapter 2. Solving Linear Equations

32. In geometry, a _____ of a circle is any straight line segment that passes through the center of the circle and whose endpoints are on the circle. The diameters are the longest chords of the circle. The word '_____' derives from Greek διἀ¬μετρος , 'diagonal of a circle', from δια- (dia-), 'across, through' + μἰτρον (metron), 'a measure'.)
   a. -module
   b. 2-bridge knot
   c. -equivalence
   d. Diameter

33. In linear algebra and the theory of matrices, the _____ of a matrix block (i.e., a submatrix within a larger matrix) is defined as follows. Suppose A, B, C, D are respectively p×p, p×q, q×p and q×q matrices, and D is invertible. Let

$$M = \begin{bmatrix} A & B \\ C & D \end{bmatrix}$$

so that M is a (p+q)×(p+q) matrix.

   a. Homogeneous function
   b. Schur complement
   c. Projection-valued measure
   d. Fundamental theorem of linear algebra

34. In discrete mathematics and predominantly in set theory, a _____ is a concept used in comparisons of sets to refer to the unique values of one set in relation to another. The terms 'absolute' and 'relative' _____ refer to more specific applications of the concept, with universal complements referring to elements unique to the universal set and the latter referring to the unique elements of one set in relation to another. In this image, the universal set is represented by the border of the image, and the set A as a disc.
   a. Pointed set
   b. -equivalence
   c. -module
   d. Complement

35. where B is the _____ of the product. To remove A_1 from the product, we can then write

$$\mathbf{A}_1^{-1}(\mathbf{A}_1\mathbf{A}_2\cdots\mathbf{A}_n)\mathbf{B} = \mathbf{A}_1^{-1}\mathbf{I}$$

which would reduce the equation to

$$(\mathbf{A}_2\mathbf{A}_3\cdots\mathbf{A}_n)\mathbf{B} = \mathbf{A}_1^{-1}\mathbf{I}.$$

Likewise, then, from

$$\mathbf{A}_2^{-1}(\mathbf{A}_2\mathbf{A}_3\cdots\mathbf{A}_n)\mathbf{B} = \mathbf{A}_2^{-1}\mathbf{A}_1^{-1}\mathbf{I}$$

which simplifies to

$$(\mathbf{A}_3\mathbf{A}_4\cdots\mathbf{A}_n)\mathbf{B} = \mathbf{A}_2^{-1}\mathbf{A}_1^{-1}\mathbf{I}.$$

If one repeat the process up to A_n, the equation becomes

$$B = A_n^{-1}A_{n-1}^{-1}\cdots A_2^{-1}A_1^{-1}I$$

$$B = A_n^{-1}A_{n-1}^{-1}\cdots A_2^{-1}A_1^{-1}$$

but B is the _____, i.e. $B = (A_1 A_2 \cdots A_n)^{-1}$ so the property is established.

Over the field of real numbers, the set of singular n-by-n matrices, considered as a subset of $R^{n\times n}$, is a null set, i.e., has Lebesgue measure zero.

a. AKS primality test
c. ADE classification
b. Inverse matrix
d. Abelian P-root group

36. Let S be a set with a binary operation *. If e is an identity element of (S, *) and a * b = e, then a is called a _____ of b and b is called a right inverse of a. If an element x is both a _____ and a right inverse of y, then x is called a two-sided inverse, or simply an inverse, of y.

a. 2-bridge knot
c. -equivalence
b. -module
d. Left inverse

37. Matrix inversion is the process of finding the matrix B that satisfies the prior equation for a given _____ A.

a. Independent equation
c. Invertible matrix
b. Orientation
d. Overdetermined

38. In linear algebra, a _____ is a square matrix in which the entries outside the main diagonal (â†") are all zero. The diagonal entries themselves may or may not be zero. Thus, the matrix D = ($d_{i,j}$) with n columns and n rows is diagonal if:

$$d_{i,j} = 0 \text{ if } i \neq j \quad \forall i,j \in \{1,2,\ldots,n\}.$$

For example, the following matrix is diagonal:

$$\begin{bmatrix} 1 & 0 & 0 \\ 0 & 4 & 0 \\ 0 & 0 & -3 \end{bmatrix}.$$

The term _____ may sometimes refer to a rectangular _____, which is an m-by-n matrix with only the entries of the form $d_{i,i}$ possibly non-zero; for example,

$$\begin{bmatrix} 1 & 0 & 0 \\ 0 & 4 & 0 \\ 0 & 0 & -3 \\ 0 & 0 & 0 \end{bmatrix}, \text{ or}$$

a. Hessenberg matrix
b. Matrix representation
c. Diagonal matrix
d. Levinson recursion

39. In linear algebra a matrix is in _____ if

- All nonzero rows are above any rows of all zeroes, and
- The leading coefficient (also called pivot) of a row is always strictly to the right of the leading coefficient of the row above it.

Some texts add a third condition:

- The leading coefficient of each nonzero row is one.

A matrix is in reduced _____ if it satisfies the above three conditions, and if, in addition

- Every leading coefficient is 1 and is the only nonzero entry in its column.

The first non-zero entry in each row is called a pivot.

This matrix is in reduced _____:

$$\begin{bmatrix} 1 & 0 & 0 & 0 & 0 \\ 0 & 1 & 0 & 0 & 0 \\ 0 & 0 & 1 & 0 & 0 \\ 0 & 0 & 0 & 1 & 0 \end{bmatrix}$$

The following matrix is also in _____, but not in reduced row form:

$$\begin{bmatrix} 1 & 9 & 1 & 1 \\ 0 & 1 & 0 & 2 \\ 0 & 0 & 1 & 3 \end{bmatrix}$$

However, this matrix is not in _____, as the leading coefficient of row 3 is not strictly to the right of the leading coefficient of row 2, and the main diagonal is not made up of only ones.

$$\begin{bmatrix} 1 & 2 & 3 & 4 \\ 0 & 3 & 7 & 2 \\ 0 & 2 & 0 & 0 \end{bmatrix}$$

Every non-zero matrix can be reduced to an infinite number of echelon forms (they can all be multiples of each other, for example) via elementary matrix transformations.

a. -equivalence
c. -module
b. 2-bridge knot
d. Row echelon form

40. The _____ of an m-by-n matrix with real entries is the subspace of R^n generated by the row vectors of the matrix. Its dimension is equal to the rank of the matrix and is at most min(m,n.)

The column space of an m-by-n matrix with real entries is the subspace of R^m generated by the column vectors of the matrix.

a. Goodman-Nguyen-van Fraassen algebra
c. Row space
b. Differential graded algebra
d. Restriction of scalars

41. In linear algebra, a _____ matrix is a matrix that is 'almost' a diagonal matrix. To be exact: a _____ matrix has nonzero elements only in the main diagonal, the first diagonal below this, and the first diagonal above the main diagonal.

For example, the following matrix is _____:

$$\begin{pmatrix} 1 & 4 & 0 & 0 \\ 3 & 4 & 1 & 0 \\ 0 & 2 & 3 & 4 \\ 0 & 0 & 1 & 3 \end{pmatrix}.$$

A determinant formed from a _____ matrix is known as a continuant.

a. -equivalence
c. Tridiagonal
b. -module
d. 2-bridge knot

42. In linear algebra, a _____ is a matrix that is 'almost' a diagonal matrix. To be exact: a _____ has nonzero elements only in the main diagonal, the first diagonal below this, and the first diagonal above the main diagonal.

For example, the following matrix is tridiagonal:

$$\begin{pmatrix} 1 & 4 & 0 & 0 \\ 3 & 4 & 1 & 0 \\ 0 & 2 & 3 & 4 \\ 0 & 0 & 1 & 3 \end{pmatrix}.$$

A determinant formed from a _____ is known as a continuant.

a. Diagonalizable matrix
b. Tridiagonal matrix
c. Similar
d. Wilkinson matrices

43. In linear algebra, a _____ is a square matrix with entries being the unit fractions

$$H_{ij} = \frac{1}{i+j-1}.$$

For example, this is the 5 × 5 _____:

$$H = \begin{bmatrix} 1 & \frac{1}{2} & \frac{1}{3} & \frac{1}{4} & \frac{1}{5} \\ \frac{1}{2} & \frac{1}{3} & \frac{1}{4} & \frac{1}{5} & \frac{1}{6} \\ \frac{1}{3} & \frac{1}{4} & \frac{1}{5} & \frac{1}{6} & \frac{1}{7} \\ \frac{1}{4} & \frac{1}{5} & \frac{1}{6} & \frac{1}{7} & \frac{1}{8} \\ \frac{1}{5} & \frac{1}{6} & \frac{1}{7} & \frac{1}{8} & \frac{1}{9} \end{bmatrix}.$$

The _____ can be regarded as derived from the integral

$$H_{ij} = \int_0^1 x^{i+j-2}\, dx,$$

that is, as a Gramian matrix for powers of x. It arises in the least squares approximation of arbitrary functions by polynomials.

The Hilbert matrices are canonical examples of ill-conditioned matrices, making them notoriously difficult to use in numerical computation.

a. Diagonally dominant
b. Minimum degree algorithm
c. Triangular matrix
d. Hilbert matrix

44. In mathematics, _____ or factoring is the decomposition of an object ' href='/wiki/Matrix_(mathematics)'>matrix) into a product of other objects, or factors, which when multiplied together give the original. For example, the number 15 factors into primes as 3 × 5, and the polynomial $x^2 - 4$ factors as (x − 2)(x + 2.) In all cases, a product of simpler objects is obtained.
a. Factorization
b. 2-bridge knot
c. -equivalence
d. -module

45. In its simplest meaning in mathematics and logic, an _____ is an action or procedure which produces a new value from one or more input values. There are two common types of operations: unary and binary. Unary operations involve only one value, such as negation and trigonometric functions.

a. ADE classification
b. AKS primality test
c. Abelian P-root group
d. Operation

46. In mathematics, the _____, denoted by ⊗, may be applied in different contexts to vectors, matrices, tensors, vector spaces, algebras, topological vector spaces, and modules. In each case the significance of the symbol is the same: the most general bilinear operation. In some contexts, this product is also referred to as outer product.
   a. Cycle graph
   b. Linear span
   c. Near-semiring
   d. Tensor product

47. In linear algebra, the _____ of a matrix A is another matrix A^T (also written A′, A^{tr} or ^tA) created by any one of the following equivalent actions:

   - write the rows of A as the columns of A^T
   - write the columns of A as the rows of A^T
   - reflect A by its main diagonal (which starts from the top left) to obtain A^T

   Formally, the _____ of an m × n matrix A with elements A_{ij} is the n × m matrix

   $$A^T_{ij} = A_{ji} \text{ for } 1 \leq i \leq n, 1 \leq j \leq m.$$

   The _____ of a scalar is the same scalar.

   - $\begin{bmatrix} 1 & 2 \end{bmatrix}^T = \begin{bmatrix} 1 \\ 2 \end{bmatrix}.$

   - $\begin{bmatrix} 1 & 2 \\ 3 & 4 \end{bmatrix}^T = \begin{bmatrix} 1 & 3 \\ 2 & 4 \end{bmatrix}.$

   - $\begin{bmatrix} 1 & 2 \\ 3 & 4 \\ 5 & 6 \end{bmatrix}^T = \begin{bmatrix} 1 & 3 & 5 \\ 2 & 4 & 6 \end{bmatrix}.$

   For matrices A, B and scalar c we have the following properties of _____:

   1. $(A^T)^T = A$

      Taking the _____ is an involution (self inverse.)

   - $(A + B)^T = A^T + B^T$

      The _____ respects addition.

   - $(AB)^T = B^T A^T$

Note that the order of the factors reverses. From this one can deduce that a square matrix A is invertible if and only if A^T is invertible, and in this case we have (A^{-1})^T = (A^T)$^{-1}$. It is relatively easy to extend this result to the general case of multiple matrices, where we find that (ABC...XYZ)^T = Z^{T}Y^{T}X^T...C^{T}B^{T}A^T.

- $(c\mathbf{A})^T = c\mathbf{A}^T$

    The _____ of a scalar is the same scalar. Together with (2), this states that the _____ is a linear map from the space of m × n matrices to the space of all n × m matrices.

- $\det(\mathbf{A}^T) = \det(\mathbf{A})$

    The determinant of a square matrix is the same as that of its _____.

- The dot product of two column vectors a and b can be computed as

$$\mathbf{a} \cdot \mathbf{b} = \mathbf{a}^T \mathbf{b},$$

which is written as $a_i b^i$ in Einstein notation.
- If A has only real entries, then A^{T}A is a positive-semidefinite matrix.
- $(\mathbf{A}^T)^{-1} = (\mathbf{A}^{-1})^T$

    The _____ of an invertible matrix is also invertible, and its inverse is the _____ of the inverse of the original matrix.

- If A is a square matrix, then its eigenvalues are equal to the eigenvalues of its _____.

A square matrix whose _____ is equal to itself is called a symmetric matrix; that is, A is symmetric if

$$\mathbf{A}^T = \mathbf{A}.$$

A square matrix whose _____ is also its inverse is called an orthogonal matrix; that is, G is orthogonal if

$$\mathbf{G}\mathbf{G}^T = \mathbf{G}^T\mathbf{G} = \mathbf{I}_n, \text{ the identity matrix, i.e. } G^T = G^{-1}.$$

Chapter 2. Solving Linear Equations

A square matrix whose _____ is equal to its negative is called skew-symmetric matrix; that is, A is skew-symmetric if

$$\mathbf{A}^T = -\mathbf{A}.$$

The conjugate _____ of the complex matrix A, written as A*, is obtained by taking the _____ of A and the complex conjugate of each entry:

$$\mathbf{A}^* = (\overline{\mathbf{A}})^T = \overline{(\mathbf{A}^T)}.$$

If f: V→W is a linear map between vector spaces V and W with nondegenerate bilinear forms, we define the _____ of f to be the linear map $^t f$: W→V, determined by

$$B_V(v, {}^t f(w)) = B_W(f(v), w) \quad \forall \, v \in V, w \in W.$$

Here, B_V and B_W are the bilinear forms on V and W respectively. The matrix of the _____ of a map is the transposed matrix only if the bases are orthonormal with respect to their bilinear forms.

Over a complex vector space, one often works with sesquilinear forms instead of bilinear (conjugate-linear in one argument.)

a. Drazin inverse
b. Levinson recursion
c. Tridiagonal matrix
d. Transpose

48. In group theory, a branch of mathematics, the term _____ is used in two closely related senses:

- the _____ of a group is its cardinality, i.e. the number of its elements;
- the _____, sometimes period, of an element a of a group is the smallest positive integer m such that a^m = e (where e denotes the identity element of the group, and a^m denotes the product of m copies of a.) If no such m exists, we say that a has infinite _____. All elements of finite groups have finite _____.

We denote the _____ of a group G by ord(G) or $|G|$ and the _____ of an element a by ord(a) or $|a|$.

Example. The symmetric group S_3 has the following multiplication table.

This group has six elements, so ord(S_3) = 6.

a. Index calculus algorithm
b. Order
c. Outer automorphism group
d. Artin group

Chapter 2. Solving Linear Equations

49. The term _____ or centre is used in various contexts in abstract algebra to denote the set of all those elements that commute with all other elements. More specifically:

- The _____ of a group G consists of all those elements x in G such that xg = gx for all g in G. This is a normal subgroup of G.
- The _____ of a ring R is the subset of R consisting of all those elements x of R such that xr = rx for all r in R. The _____ is a commutative subring of R, so R is an algebra over its _____.
- The _____ of an algebra A consists of all those elements x of A such that xa = ax for all a in A. See also: central simple algebra.
- The _____ of a Lie algebra L consists of all those elements x in L such that [x,a] = 0 for all a in L. This is an ideal of the Lie algebra L.
- The _____ of a monoidal category C consists of pairs (A,u) where A is an object of C, and $u : A \otimes - \rightarrow - \otimes A$ a natural isomorphism satisfying certain axioms.

a. Self-adjoint
c. Ring theory
b. Left alternative
d. Center

50. The set of all symmetry operations considered, on all objects in a set X, can be modeled as a group action g : G × X → X, where the image of g in G and x in X is written as gÂ·x. If, for some g, gÂ·x = y then x and y are said to be symmetrical to each other. For each object x, operations g for which gÂ·x = x form a group, the _____ of the object, a subgroup of G. If the _____ of x is the trivial group then x is said to be asymmetric, otherwise symmetric.

a. -module
c. 2-bridge knot
b. -equivalence
d. Symmetry group

51. In linear algebra, a _____ is a square matrix, A, that is equal to its transpose

$$A = A^T.$$

The entries of a _____ are symmetric with respect to the main diagonal (top left to bottom right.) So if the entries are written as A = (a_{ij}), then

$$a_{ij} = a_{ji}$$

for all indices i and j. The following 3×3 matrix is symmetric:

$$\begin{bmatrix} 1 & 2 & 3 \\ 2 & 4 & -5 \\ 3 & -5 & 6 \end{bmatrix}.$$

A matrix is called skew-symmetric or antisymmetric if its transpose is the same as its negative.

a. Stieltjes matrix
c. Zero matrix
b. Butson-type
d. Symmetric matrix

52. In the case of Gaussian elimination, it is best to choose a pivot element with large absolute value. This improves the numerical stability. In _____, the algorithm considers all entries in the column of the matrix that is currently being considered, picks the entry with largest absolute value, and finally swaps rows such that this entry is the pivot in question.
   a. Partial pivoting
   b. -module
   c. 2-bridge knot
   d. -equivalence

53. In mathematics, particularly linear algebra and functional analysis, the _____ is any of a number of results about linear operators or about matrices. In broad terms the _____ provides conditions under which an operator or a matrix can be diagonalized (that is, represented as a diagonal matrix in some basis.) This concept of diagonalization is relatively straightforward for operators on finite-dimensional spaces, but requires some modification for operators on infinite-dimensional spaces.
   a. Spectral asymmetry
   b. Spectral geometry
   c. Spectral radius
   d. Spectral theorem

54. A _____ is a set G closed under a binary operation · satisfying the following 3 axioms:

   - Associativity: For all a, b and c in G, (a · b) · c = a · (b · c).
   - Identity element: There exists an e∈G such that for all a in G, e · a = a · e = a.
   - Inverse element: For each a in G, there is an element b in G such that a · b = b · a = e, where e is an identity element.

Basic examples for groups are the integers Z with addition operation, or rational numbers without zero Q{0} with multiplication. More generally, for any ring R, the units in R form a multiplicative _____ Groups include, however, much more general structures than the above.

   a. Product of group subsets
   b. Group
   c. Grigorchuk group
   d. Nilpotent group

Chapter 3. Vector Spaces and Subspaces

1. In mathematics, a topological space is _____ or 0-dimensional, if its topological dimension is zero if it has a base consisting of clopen sets. A _____ Hausdorff space is necessarily totally disconnected, but the converse fails. However a locally compact Hausdorff space is _____ if and only if it is totally disconnected.
   a. 2-bridge knot
   b. -module
   c. -equivalence
   d. Zero-dimensional

2. In mathematics, a _____ is a rectangular array of numbers. This way, matrices can record data that depend on multiple parameters. In particular they are used to keep track of the coefficients of multiple linear equations. Matrices are closely connected to linear transformations, which are higher-dimensional analogs of linear functions, i.e., functions of the form f(x) = c Â· x, where c is a constant. This map corresponds to a _____ with one row and column, with entry c. In addition to a number of elementary, entrywise operations such as _____ addition a key notion is _____ multiplication, which displays a number of features not encountered in numbers; for example, products of matrices depend on the order of the factors, unlike products of real numbers, say, where c Â· d = d Â· c for any two numbers c and d.
   a. Polynomial expression
   b. Commutativity
   c. Heap
   d. Matrix

3. In linear algebra, the _____ of a matrix is the set of all possible linear combinations of its column vectors. The _____ of an m × n matrix is a subspace of m-dimensional Euclidean space. The dimension of the _____ is called the rank of the matrix.
   a. Pseudovector
   b. Delta operator
   c. Linear inequality
   d. Column space

4. In linear algebra, the _____ of a matrix is obtained by changing a matrix in some way.

Given the matrices A and B, where:

$$A = \begin{bmatrix} 1 & 3 & 2 \\ 2 & 0 & 1 \\ 5 & 2 & 2 \end{bmatrix}, \quad B = \begin{bmatrix} 4 \\ 3 \\ 1 \end{bmatrix}$$

Then, the _____ is written as:

$$(A|B) = \begin{bmatrix} 1 & 3 & 2 & 4 \\ 2 & 0 & 1 & 3 \\ 5 & 2 & 2 & 1 \end{bmatrix}$$

This is useful when solving systems of linear equations or the _____ may also be used to find the inverse of a matrix by combining it with the identity matrix.

Let C be a square 2×2 matrix where

$$C = \begin{bmatrix} 1 & 3 \\ -5 & 0 \end{bmatrix}$$

To find the inverse of C we create (C | I) where I is the 2×2 identity matrix.

Chapter 3. Vector Spaces and Subspaces

a. Euclidean distance matrix
b. Augmented matrix
c. Unistochastic matrix
d. Unitary matrix

5. A _____ is a symbol that stands for a value that may vary; the term usually occurs in opposition to constant, which is a symbol for a non-varying value, i.e. completely fixed or fixed in the context of use. The concepts of constants and variables are fundamental to all modern mathematics, science, engineering, and computer programming.

Much of the basic theory for which we use variables today, such as school geometry and algebra, was developed thousands of years ago, but the use of symbolic formulae and variables is only several hundreds of years old.

a. Variable
b. 2-bridge knot
c. -equivalence
d. -module

6. In linear algebra, the _____ of the monic polynomial

$$p(t) = c_0 + c_1 t + \ldots + c_{n-1} t^{n-1} + t^n$$

is the square matrix defined as

$$C(p) = \begin{bmatrix} 0 & 0 & \ldots & 0 & -c_0 \\ 1 & 0 & \ldots & 0 & -c_1 \\ 0 & 1 & \ldots & 0 & -c_2 \\ \vdots & \vdots & \vdots & \vdots & \vdots \\ 0 & 0 & \ldots & 1 & -c_{n-1} \end{bmatrix}.$$

With this convention, and writing the basis as $v_1, \ldots, v_n$, one has $Cv_i = C^{i-1} v_1 = v_{i+1}$ (for $i < n$), and v_1 generates V as a K[C]-module: C cycles basis vectors.

Some authors use the transpose of this matrix, which (dually) cycles coordinates, and is more convenient for some purposes, like linear recursive relations.

The characteristic polynomial as well as the minimal polynomial of C(p) are equal to p; in this sense, the matrix C(p) is the 'companion' of the polynomial p.

a. Matrix representation
b. Levinson recursion
c. Wilkinson matrices
d. Companion matrix

7. In mathematics, the _____ of a vector space V is the cardinality (i.e. the number of vectors) of a basis of V. It is sometimes called Hamel _____ or algebraic _____ to distinguish it from other types of _____. All bases of a vector space have equal cardinality and so the _____ of a vector space is uniquely defined. The _____ of the vector space V over the field F can be written as $\dim_F(V)$ or as [V : F], read '_____ of V over F'.

a. Dimension
b. Partial trace
c. Dual basis
d. Cofactor

Chapter 3. Vector Spaces and Subspaces

8. In geometry, two lines or planes (or a line and a plane), are considered _____ to each other if they form congruent adjacent angles (an L-shape.) The term may be used as a noun or adjective. Thus, referring to Figure 1, the line AB is the _____ to CD through the point B. Note that by definition, a line is infinitely long, and strictly speaking AB and CD in this example represent line segments of two infinitely long lines.
   - a. -equivalence
   - b. 2-bridge knot
   - c. -module
   - d. Perpendicular

9. The _____ of an m-by-n matrix with real entries is the subspace of R^n generated by the row vectors of the matrix. Its dimension is equal to the rank of the matrix and is at most min(m,n.)

The column space of an m-by-n matrix with real entries is the subspace of R^m generated by the column vectors of the matrix.

   - a. Goodman-Nguyen-van Fraassen algebra
   - b. Differential graded algebra
   - c. Restriction of scalars
   - d. Row space

10. For each _____ of a linear transformation, there is a corresponding scalar value called an eigenvalue for that vector, which determines the amount the _____ is scaled under the linear transformation. For example, an eigenvalue of +2 means that the _____ is doubled in length and points in the same direction. An eigenvalue of +1 means that the _____ is unchanged, while an eigenvalue of −1 means that the _____ is reversed in sense.
   - a. Eigenvector
   - b. AKS primality test
   - c. Abelian P-root group
   - d. ADE classification

11. In its simplest meaning in mathematics and logic, an _____ is an action or procedure which produces a new value from one or more input values. There are two common types of operations: unary and binary. Unary operations involve only one value, such as negation and trigonometric functions.
   - a. ADE classification
   - b. Abelian P-root group
   - c. AKS primality test
   - d. Operation

12. In mathematics, especially in linear algebra and matrix theory, the duplication matrix and the _____ are linear transformations used for transforming half-vectorizations of matrices into vectorizations or (respectively) vice-versa.

The duplication matrix D_n is the unique $n^2 \times n(n+1)/2$ matrix which, for any $n \times n$ symmetric matrix A, transforms vech(A) into vec(A):

$$D_n \text{ vech}(A) = \text{vec}(A.)$$

Chapter 3. Vector Spaces and Subspaces

For the 2×2 symmetric matrix $A = \begin{bmatrix} a & b \\ b & d \end{bmatrix}$, this transformation reads

$$\begin{bmatrix} 1 & 0 & 0 \\ 0 & 1 & 0 \\ 0 & 1 & 0 \\ 0 & 0 & 1 \end{bmatrix} \begin{bmatrix} a \\ b \\ d \end{bmatrix} = \begin{bmatrix} a \\ b \\ b \\ d \end{bmatrix}$$

The _____ L_n is the unique $n(n+1)/2 \times n^2$ matrix which, for any $n \times n$ matrix A, transforms vec(A) into vech(A):

$$L_n \text{vec}(A) = \text{vech}(A.)$$

a. AKS primality test
c. Elimination matrix
b. Abelian P-root group
d. ADE classification

13. The column _____ of a matrix A is the maximal number of linearly independent columns of A. Likewise, the row _____ is the maximal number of linearly independent rows of A.

Since the column _____ and the row _____ are always equal, they are simply called the _____ of A. More abstractly, it is the dimension of the image of A. For the proofs, see, e.g., Murase (1960), Andrea ' Wong (1960), Williams ' Cater (1968), Mackiw (1995.) It is commonly denoted by either rk(A) or _____ A.

a. Split-complex number
c. Rank
b. Generalized Pauli matrices
d. Schur complement

14. In mathematics, a _____ is a matrix formed by selecting certain rows and columns from a bigger matrix. That is, as an array, it is cut down to those entries constrained by row and column.

For example

$$\mathbf{A} = \begin{bmatrix} a_{11} & a_{12} & a_{13} & a_{14} \\ a_{21} & a_{22} & a_{23} & a_{24} \\ a_{31} & a_{32} & a_{33} & a_{34} \end{bmatrix}.$$

Then

$$\mathbf{A}[1,2;1,3,4] = \begin{bmatrix} a_{11} & a_{13} & a_{14} \\ a_{21} & a_{23} & a_{24} \end{bmatrix}$$

Chapter 3. Vector Spaces and Subspaces

is a _____ of A formed by rows 1,2 and columns 1,3,4.

a. Submatrix
c. Lie product formula
b. Quasideterminant
d. Smith normal form

15. In linear algebra, functional analysis and related areas of mathematics, a _____ is a function that assigns a strictly positive length or size to all vectors in a vector space, other than the zero vector. A seminorm (or pseudonorm), on the other hand, is allowed to assign zero length to some non-zero vectors.

A simple example is the 2-dimensional Euclidean space R^2 equipped with the Euclidean _____.

a. Quasinorm
c. -module
b. -equivalence
d. Norm

16. In linear algebra, a family of vectors is _____ if none of them can be written as a linear combination of finitely many other vectors in the collection. A family of vectors which is not _____ is called linearly dependent. For instance, in the three-dimensional real vector space $\mathbb{R}^3$ we have the following example.

a. Composition ring
c. Grothendieck group
b. Derivative algebra
d. Linearly independent

17. In linear algebra, a _____ is a set of vectors that, in a linear combination, can represent every vector in a given vector space or free module, and such that no element of the set can be represented as a linear combination of the others. In other words, a _____ is a linearly independent spanning set.

a. Minor
c. Supergroup
b. Chirality
d. Basis

18. In mathematics, the _____ for a Euclidean space consists of one unit vector pointing in the direction of each axis of the Cartesian coordinate system. For example, the _____ for the Euclidean plane are the vectors

$$\mathbf{e}_x = (1,0), \quad \mathbf{e}_y = (0,1),$$

and the _____ for three-dimensional space are the vectors

$$\mathbf{e}_x = (1,0,0), \quad \mathbf{e}_y = (0,1,0), \quad \mathbf{e}_z = (0,0,1).$$

Here the vector e_x points in the x direction, the vector e_y points in the y direction, and the vector e_z points in the z direction. There are several common notations for these vectors, including {e_x, e_y, e_z}, {e_1, e_2, e_3}, {i, j, k}, and {x, y, z}.

a. -module
c. 2-bridge knot
b. Standard basis
d. -equivalence

Chapter 3. Vector Spaces and Subspaces

19. Let S be a set with a binary operation * . If e is an identity element of (S, *) and a * b = e, then a is called a _____ of b and b is called a right inverse of a. If an element x is both a _____ and a right inverse of y, then x is called a two-sided inverse, or simply an inverse, of y.
    a. 2-bridge knot
    b. -module
    c. -equivalence
    d. Left inverse

20. Matrix inversion is the process of finding the matrix B that satisfies the prior equation for a given _____ A.
    a. Independent equation
    b. Overdetermined
    c. Orientation
    d. Invertible matrix

21. In mathematics, and more specifically set theory, the _____ is the unique set having no (zero) members. Some axiomatic set theories assure that the _____ exists by including an axiom of _____; in other theories, its existence can be deduced. Many possible properties of sets are trivially true for the _____.
    a. AKS primality test
    b. ADE classification
    c. Abelian P-root group
    d. Empty set

22. In mathematics, a _____ is a set of functions of a given kind from a set X to a set Y. It is called a space because in many applications, it is a topological space or a vector space or both.

Function spaces appear in various areas of mathematics:

- in set theory, the power set of a set X may be identified with the set of all functions from X to {0,1};, denoted 2^X. More generally, the set of functions $X \rightarrow Y$ is denoted Y^X.

- in linear algebra the set of all linear transformations from a vector space V to another one, W, over the same field, is itself a vector space;

- in functional analysis the same is seen for continuous linear transformations, including topologies on the vector spaces in the above, and many of the major examples are function spaces carrying a topology; the best known examples include Hilbert spaces and Banach spaces.

- in functional analysis the set of all functions from the natural numbers to some set X is called a sequence space. It consists of the set of all possible sequences of elements of X.

- in topology, one may attempt to put a topology on the space of continuous functions from a topological space X to another one Y, with utility depending on the nature of the spaces. A commonly used example is the compact-open topology, e.g. loop space.

    a. -module
    b. -equivalence
    c. 2-bridge knot
    d. Function space

23. In several fields of mathematics the term _____ is used with different but closely related meanings. They all relate to the notion of mapping the elements of a set to other elements of the same set, i.e., exchanging (or 'permuting') elements of a set.

Chapter 3. Vector Spaces and Subspaces

The general concept of _____ can be defined more formally in different contexts:

In combinatorics, a _____ is usually understood to be a sequence containing each element from a finite set once, and only once.

a. Rupture field
b. Permutation
c. Near-field
d. Binary function

24. In mathematics, in matrix theory, a _____ is a square (0,1)-matrix that has exactly one entry 1 in each row and each column and 0's elsewhere. Each such matrix represents a specific permutation of m elements and, when used to multiply another matrix, can produce that permutation in the rows or columns of the other matrix.

Given a permutation π of m elements,

$$\pi : \{1, \ldots, m\} \to \{1, \ldots, m\}$$

given in two-line form by

$$\begin{pmatrix} 1 & 2 & \cdots & m \\ \pi(1) & \pi(2) & \cdots & \pi(m) \end{pmatrix},$$

its _____ is the m × m matrix P_π whose entries are all 0 except that in row i, the entry π(i) equals 1.

a. Skew-symmetric
b. Permutation matrix
c. Main diagonal
d. Hessenberg matrix

25. In mathematics, a _____ is a binary matrix with ones only on the superdiagonal or subdiagonal, and zeroes elsewhere. A _____ U with ones on the superdiagonal is an upper _____. The alternative subdiagonal matrix L is unsurprisingly known as a lower _____.

a. Shift matrix
b. Hamiltonian matrix
c. Jacket matrix
d. Binary matrix

Chapter 4. Orthogonality

1. In mathematics, two vectors are _____ if they are perpendicular, i.e., they form a right angle. The word comes from the Greek ἀ½€ρθΐŒς , meaning 'straight', and γωνῑα (gonia), meaning 'angle'. For example, a subway and the street above, although they do not physically intersect, are _____ if they cross at a right angle.
   a. Embedding
   b. Expression
   c. Unital
   d. Orthogonal

2. Definition. Two vector subspaces A and B of an inner product space V are called _____ if each vector in A is orthogonal to each vector in B. The largest subspace that is orthogonal to a given subspace is its orthogonal complement.
   a. Orthogonal subspaces
   b. ADE classification
   c. Abelian P-root group
   d. AKS primality test

3. In geometry, two lines or planes (or a line and a plane), are considered _____ to each other if they form congruent adjacent angles (an L-shape.) The term may be used as a noun or adjective. Thus, referring to Figure 1, the line AB is the _____ to CD through the point B. Note that by definition, a line is infinitely long, and strictly speaking AB and CD in this example represent line segments of two infinitely long lines.
   a. -module
   b. Perpendicular
   c. 2-bridge knot
   d. -equivalence

4. In the mathematical fields of linear algebra and functional analysis, the _____ $W^\perp$ of a subspace W of an inner product space V is the set of all vectors in V that are orthogonal to every vector in W, i.e., it is

$$W^\perp = \{x \in V : \langle x, y \rangle = 0 \text{ for all } y \in W\}.$$

Informally, it is called the perp, short for perpendicular complement.

The _____ is always closed in the metric topology. In finite-dimensional spaces, that is merely an instance of the fact that all subspaces of a vector space are closed.

   a. Euclidean subspace
   b. Independent equation
   c. Invariant subspace
   d. Orthogonal complement

5. In mathematics, a generalized inverse or _____ of a matrix A is a matrix that has some properties of the inverse matrix of A but not necessarily all of them. The term 'the _____' commonly means the Moore-Penrose _____.

The purpose of constructing a generalized inverse is to obtain a matrix that can serve as the inverse in some sense for a wider class of matrices than invertible ones.

   a. -module
   b. 2-bridge knot
   c. -equivalence
   d. Pseudoinverse

6. In discrete mathematics and predominantly in set theory, a _____ is a concept used in comparisons of sets to refer to the unique values of one set in relation to another. The terms 'absolute' and 'relative' _____ refer to more specific applications of the concept, with universal complements referring to elements unique to the universal set and the latter referring to the unique elements of one set in relation to another. In this image, the universal set is represented by the border of the image, and the set A as a disc.

a. -module
b. -equivalence
c. Pointed set
d. Complement

7. In linear algebra, a _____ is a set of vectors that, in a linear combination, can represent every vector in a given vector space or free module, and such that no element of the set can be represented as a linear combination of the others. In other words, a _____ is a linearly independent spanning set.
   a. Basis
   b. Minor
   c. Chirality
   d. Supergroup

8. In mathematics, particularly linear algebra, a _____ is a matrix with all its entries being zero. Some examples of zero matrices are

$$0_{1,1} = \begin{bmatrix} 0 \end{bmatrix}, \ 0_{2,2} = \begin{bmatrix} 0 & 0 \\ 0 & 0 \end{bmatrix}, \ 0_{2,3} = \begin{bmatrix} 0 & 0 & 0 \\ 0 & 0 & 0 \end{bmatrix},$$

The set of m×n matrices with entries in a ring K forms a ring $K_{m,n}$. The _____ $0_{K_{m,n}}$ in $K_{m,n}$ is the matrix with all entries equal to 0_K, where 0_K is the additive identity in K.

   a. Normal matrix
   b. Regular Hadamard matrix
   c. Complex Hadamard matrix
   d. Zero matrix

9. For each _____ of a linear transformation, there is a corresponding scalar value called an eigenvalue for that vector, which determines the amount the _____ is scaled under the linear transformation. For example, an eigenvalue of +2 means that the _____ is doubled in length and points in the same direction. An eigenvalue of +1 means that the _____ is unchanged, while an eigenvalue of −1 means that the _____ is reversed in sense.
   a. Eigenvector
   b. ADE classification
   c. Abelian P-root group
   d. AKS primality test

10. In mathematics, a _____ is a rectangular array of numbers. This way, matrices can record data that depend on multiple parameters. In particular they are used to keep track of the coefficients of multiple linear equations. Matrices are closely connected to linear transformations, which are higher-dimensional analogs of linear functions, i.e., functions of the form f(x) = c Â· x, where c is a constant. This map corresponds to a _____ with one row and column, with entry c. In addition to a number of elementary, entrywise operations such as _____ addition a key notion is _____ multiplication, which displays a number of features not encountered in numbers; for example, products of matrices depend on the order of the factors, unlike products of real numbers, say, where c Â· d = d Â· c for any two numbers c and d.
    a. Commutativity
    b. Polynomial expression
    c. Matrix
    d. Heap

11. In linear algebra and functional analysis, a _____ is a linear transformation P from a vector space to itself such that $P^2 = P$. It leaves its image unchanged. Though abstract, this definition of '_____' formalizes and generalizes the idea of graphical _____.
    a. C_0-semigroup
    b. Projection
    c. Convolution power
    d. Lumer-Phillips theorem

Chapter 4. Orthogonality

12. In geometry, a _____ is a straight curve. When geometry is used to model the real world, lines are used to represent straight objects with negligible width and height. Lines are an idealisation of such objects and have no width or height at all and are usually considered to be infinitely long.
   - a. Line
   - b. -equivalence
   - c. -module
   - d. 2-bridge knot

13. In mathematics, the _____ of a vector space V is the cardinality (i.e. the number of vectors) of a basis of V. It is sometimes called Hamel _____ or algebraic _____ to distinguish it from other types of _____. All bases of a vector space have equal cardinality and so the _____ of a vector space is uniquely defined. The _____ of the vector space V over the field F can be written as $\dim_F(V)$ or as [V : F], read '_____ of V over F'.
   - a. Dual basis
   - b. Partial trace
   - c. Cofactor
   - d. Dimension

14. The column _____ of a matrix A is the maximal number of linearly independent columns of A. Likewise, the row _____ is the maximal number of linearly independent rows of A.

    Since the column _____ and the row _____ are always equal, they are simply called the _____ of A. More abstractly, it is the dimension of the image of A. For the proofs, see, e.g., Murase (1960), Andrea ' Wong (1960), Williams ' Cater (1968), Mackiw (1995).) It is commonly denoted by either rk(A) or _____ A.

   - a. Split-complex number
   - b. Schur complement
   - c. Generalized Pauli matrices
   - d. Rank

15. The _____ magnitude or Error vectorM is a measure used to quantify the performance of a digital radio transmitter or receiver. A signal sent by an ideal transmitter or received by a receiver would have all constellation points precisely at the ideal locations, however various imperfections in the implementation cause the actual constellation points to deviate from the ideal locations.
   - a. ADE classification
   - b. Abelian P-root group
   - c. Error vector
   - d. AKS primality test

16. The _____ is an efficient recursive filter that estimates the state of a linear dynamic system from a series of noisy measurements. It is used in a wide range of engineering applications from radar to computer vision, and is an important topic in control theory and control systems engineering. Together with the linear-quadratic regulator (LQR), the _____ solves the linear-quadratic-Gaussian control problem (LQG).
   - a. -equivalence
   - b. 2-bridge knot
   - c. Kalman filter
   - d. -module

17. The method of _____ is used to approximately solve overdetermined systems, i.e. systems of equations in which there are more equations than unknowns. _____ is often applied in statistical contexts, particularly regression analysis.

    _____ can be interpreted as a method of fitting data.

   - a. 2-bridge knot
   - b. -equivalence
   - c. Least squares
   - d. -module

Chapter 4. Orthogonality

18. In mathematics, the _____ is a conic section, the intersection of a right circular conical surface and a plane parallel to a generating straight line of that surface. Given a point (the focus) and a line (the directrix) that lie in a plane, the locus of points in that plane that are equidistant to them is a _____.

A particular case arises when the plane is tangent to the conical surface of a circle.

a. -module
c. 2-bridge knot
b. -equivalence
d. Parabola

19. In probability theory and statistics, a _____ is described as the number separating the higher half of a sample, a population from the lower half. The _____ of a finite list of numbers can be found by arranging all the observations from lowest value to highest value and picking the middle one. If there is an even number of observations, the _____ is not unique, so one often takes the mean of the two middle values.

a. 2-bridge knot
c. -equivalence
b. -module
d. Median

20. In probability theory and statistics, _____ is a measure of how much two variables change together (variance is a special case of the _____ when the two variables are identical.)

If two variables tend to vary together (that is, when one of them is above its expected value, then the other variable tends to be above its expected value too), then the _____ between the two variables will be positive. On the other hand, if one of them tends to be above its expected value when the other variable is below its expected value, then the _____ between the two variables will be negative.

a. -equivalence
c. Covariance
b. 2-bridge knot
d. -module

21. In statistics and probability theory, the _____ or dispersion matrix is a matrix of covariances between elements of a random vector. It is the natural generalization to higher dimensions of the concept of the variance of a scalar-valued random variable.

If entries in the column vector

$$X = \begin{bmatrix} X_1 \\ \vdots \\ X_n \end{bmatrix}$$

are random variables, each with finite variance, then the _____ Σ is the matrix whose (i, j) entry is the covariance

$$\Sigma_{ij} = \operatorname{cov}(X_i, X_j) = \mathrm{E}\big[(X_i - \mu_i)(X_j - \mu_j)\big]$$

where

$$\mu_i = E(X_i)$$

is the expected value of the ith entry in the vector X. In other words, we have

$$\Sigma = \begin{bmatrix} E[(X_1 - \mu_1)(X_1 - \mu_1)] & E[(X_1 - \mu_1)(X_2 - \mu_2)] & \cdots & E[(X_1 - \mu_1)(X_n - \mu_n)] \\ E[(X_2 - \mu_2)(X_1 - \mu_1)] & E[(X_2 - \mu_2)(X_2 - \mu_2)] & \cdots & E[(X_2 - \mu_2)(X_n - \mu_n)] \\ \vdots & \vdots & \ddots & \vdots \\ E[(X_n - \mu_n)(X_1 - \mu_1)] & E[(X_n - \mu_n)(X_2 - \mu_2)] & \cdots & E[(X_n - \mu_n)(X_n - \mu_n)] \end{bmatrix}.$$

The inverse of this matrix, Σ^{-1}, is called the inverse _____, concentration matrix or precision matrix.

a. Covariance matrix
b. -module
c. -equivalence
d. 2-bridge knot

22. In probability theory and statistics, _____ is a measure of the variability or dispersion of a population, a data set, or a probability distribution. A low _____ indicates that the data points tend to be very close to the same value (the mean), while high _____ indicates that the data are e;spread oute; over a large range of values.

For example, the average height for adult men in the United States is about 70 inches, with a _____ of around 3 inches.

a. -equivalence
b. 2-bridge knot
c. -module
d. Standard deviation

23. In linear algebra, two vectors in an inner product space are _____ if they are orthogonal and both of unit length. A set of vectors form an _____ set if all vectors in the set are mutually orthogonal and all of unit length. An _____ set which forms a basis is called an _____ basis.

a. Elementary matrix
b. Orthonormal
c. Overdetermined
d. Invertible matrix

24. In mathematics, a _____ in a (unital) ring R is an invertible element of R, i.e. an element u such that there is a v in R with

$$uv = vu = 1_R,$$ where 1_R is the multiplicative identity element.

That is, u is an invertible element of the multiplicative monoid of R. If $0 \neq 1$ in the ring, then 0 is not a _____.

Unfortunately, the term _____ is also used to refer to the identity element 1_R of the ring, in expressions like ring with a _____ or _____ ring, and also e.g. '_____' matrix.

a. Ascending chain condition on principal ideals
b. Unit
c. Ore condition
d. Ore extension

25. In linear algebra, an _____ is a square matrix with real entries whose columns (or rows) are orthogonal unit vectors (i.e., orthonormal.) Equivalently, a matrix Q is orthogonal if its transpose is equal to its inverse:

$$Q^T Q = Q Q^T = I.$$

As a linear transformation, an _____ preserves the dot product of vectors, and therefore acts as an isometry of Euclidean space, such as a rotation or reflection.

The set of n × n orthogonal matrices forms a group O(n), known as the orthogonal group.

a. Unistochastic matrix
b. Orthogonal matrix
c. Alternating sign matrix
d. Unimodular matrix

26. In several fields of mathematics the term _____ is used with different but closely related meanings. They all relate to the notion of mapping the elements of a set to other elements of the same set, i.e., exchanging (or 'permuting') elements of a set.

The general concept of _____ can be defined more formally in different contexts:

In combinatorics, a _____ is usually understood to be a sequence containing each element from a finite set once, and only once.

a. Permutation
b. Binary function
c. Rupture field
d. Near-field

27. In mathematics, in matrix theory, a _____ is a square (0,1)-matrix that has exactly one entry 1 in each row and each column and 0's elsewhere. Each such matrix represents a specific permutation of m elements and, when used to multiply another matrix, can produce that permutation in the rows or columns of the other matrix.

Given a permutation π of m elements,

$$\pi : \{1, \ldots, m\} \to \{1, \ldots, m\}$$

given in two-line form by

$$\begin{pmatrix} 1 & 2 & \cdots & m \\ \pi(1) & \pi(2) & \cdots & \pi(m) \end{pmatrix},$$

its _____ is the m × m matrix P_π whose entries are all 0 except that in row i, the entry π(i) equals 1.

a. Skew-symmetric
c. Hessenberg matrix
b. Main diagonal
d. Permutation matrix

28. In linear algebra, a _____ is a linear transformation that squares to the identity ($R^2 = I$, where R is in K dimensional space), also known as an involution in the general linear group. In addition to reflections across hyperplanes, the class of general reflections includes point reflections, reflections across subspaces of intermediate dimension, and non-orthogonal reflections.

A _____ over a hyperplane in an inner product space is necessarily symmetric, but a general _____ need not be as the example $\begin{bmatrix} 1 & 0 \\ 1 & -1 \end{bmatrix}$ shows.

a. Homomorphic secret sharing
c. Morphism
b. Reflection
d. Shear mappings

29. In geometry and linear algebra, a _____ is a transformation in a plane or in space that describes the motion of a rigid body around a fixed point. A _____ is different from a translation, which has no fixed points, and from a reflection, which 'flips' the bodies it is transforming. A _____ and the above-mentioned transformations are isometries; they leave the distance between any two points unchanged after the transformation.

a. Real matrices
c. Shear mappings
b. Rotation
d. Reflection

30. In linear algebra, a _____ is any matrix that acts as a rotation of Euclidean space. For example, the matrix

$$\begin{bmatrix} \cos\theta & -\sin\theta \\ \sin\theta & \cos\theta \end{bmatrix}$$

rotates vectors in the plane counterclockwise by an angle of θ. In three dimensions, rotation matrices are among the simplest algebraic descriptions of rotations, and are used extensively for computations in geometry, physics, and computer graphics.

a. 9-j symbols
c. Rotation matrix
b. Rotational symmetry
d. Spin magnetic moment

31. In mathematics, a _____ decomposes a periodic function or periodic signal into a sum of simple oscillating functions, namely sines and cosines. The study of _____ is a branch of Fourier analysis. _____ were introduced by Joseph Fourier (1768-1830) for the purpose of solving the heat equation in a metal plate.

Chapter 4. Orthogonality

a. -equivalence
c. Fourier series
b. -module
d. 2-bridge knot

32. In field theory, given a field extension E / F and an element α of E which is an algebraic element over F, the _____ of α is the monic polynomial p, with coefficients in F, of least degree such that p(α) = 0. The _____ is irreducible over F, and any other non-zero polynomial f with f(α) = 0 is a (polynomial) multiple of p.

For example, for $F = \mathbb{Q}, E = \mathbb{R}, \alpha = \sqrt{2}$ the _____ for α is p(x) = x^2 − 2.

a. Vandermonde polynomial
c. Ring of symmetric functions
b. Kazhdan-Lusztig polynomials
d. Minimal polynomial

33. In mathematics, a _____ is a square matrix whose entries are either +1 or −1 and whose rows are mutually orthogonal. In geometric terms, this means that every two different rows in a _____ represent two perpendicular vectors, while in combinatorial terms, it means that every two different rows have matching entries in exactly half of their columns and mismatched entries in the remaining columns. It is a consequence of this definition that the corresponding properties hold for columns as well as rows.

a. 2-bridge knot
c. -equivalence
b. -module
d. Hadamard matrix

Chapter 5. Determinants

1. In algebra, a _____ is a function depending on n that associates a scalar, det(A), to an n×n square matrix A. The fundamental geometric meaning of a _____ is a scale factor for measure when A is regarded as a linear transformation. Determinants are important both in calculus, where they enter the substitution rule for several variables, and in multilinear algebra.

   For a fixed nonnegative integer n, there is a unique _____ function for the n×n matrices over any commutative ring R. In particular, this function exists when R is the field of real or complex numbers.

   a. Functional determinant
   b. Determinant
   c. Leibniz formula
   d. Pfaffian

2. is called _____ matrix or right triangular matrix.

   The standard operations on triangular matrices conveniently preserve the triangular form: the sum and product of two _____ matrices is again _____. The inverse of an _____ matrix is also _____, and of course we can multiply an _____ matrix by a constant and it will still be _____.

   a. Abelian P-root group
   b. ADE classification
   c. AKS primality test
   d. Upper triangular

3. is called _____ or right triangular matrix.

   The standard operations on triangular matrices conveniently preserve the triangular form: the sum and product of two upper triangular matrices is again upper triangular. The inverse of an _____ is also upper triangular, and of course we can multiply an _____ by a constant and it will still be upper triangular.

   a. ADE classification
   b. Abelian P-root group
   c. AKS primality test
   d. Upper triangular matrix

4. In geometry, a _____ is a straight curve. When geometry is used to model the real world, lines are used to represent straight objects with negligible width and height. Lines are an idealisation of such objects and have no width or height at all and are usually considered to be infinitely long.
   a. -equivalence
   b. 2-bridge knot
   c. -module
   d. Line

5. In mathematics, a _____ is a rectangular array of numbers. This way, matrices can record data that depend on multiple parameters. In particular they are used to keep track of the coefficients of multiple linear equations. Matrices are closely connected to linear transformations, which are higher-dimensional analogs of linear functions, i.e., functions of the form f(x) = c Â· x, where c is a constant. This map corresponds to a _____ with one row and column, with entry c. In addition to a number of elementary, entrywise operations such as _____ addition a key notion is _____ multiplication, which displays a number of features not encountered in numbers; for example, products of matrices depend on the order of the factors, unlike products of real numbers, say, where c Â· d = d Â· c for any two numbers c and d.
   a. Commutativity
   b. Polynomial expression
   c. Matrix
   d. Heap

Chapter 5. Determinants

6. In the mathematical discipline of linear algebra, a _____ is a special kind of square matrix where the entries either below or above the main diagonal are zero. Because matrix equations with triangular matrices are easier to solve they are very important in numerical analysis. The LU decomposition gives an algorithm to decompose any invertible matrix A into a normed lower triangle matrix L and an upper triangle matrix U.
   a. Diagonally dominant
   b. Circulant matrix
   c. Triangular matrix
   d. Hilbert matrix

7. In mathematics, two vectors are _____ if they are perpendicular, i.e., they form a right angle. The word comes from the Greek ἀ½€ρθÏŒς , meaning 'straight', and γωνῖα (gonia), meaning 'angle'. For example, a subway and the street above, although they do not physically intersect, are _____ if they cross at a right angle.
   a. Unital
   b. Orthogonal
   c. Embedding
   d. Expression

8. In linear algebra, an _____ is a square matrix with real entries whose columns (or rows) are orthogonal unit vectors (i.e., orthonormal.) Equivalently, a matrix Q is orthogonal if its transpose is equal to its inverse:

$$Q^T Q = Q Q^T = I.$$

As a linear transformation, an _____ preserves the dot product of vectors, and therefore acts as an isometry of Euclidean space, such as a rotation or reflection.

The set of n × n orthogonal matrices forms a group O(n), known as the orthogonal group.

   a. Alternating sign matrix
   b. Unistochastic matrix
   c. Unimodular matrix
   d. Orthogonal matrix

9. In linear algebra, the _____ or unit matrix of size n is the n-by-n square matrix with ones on the main diagonal and zeros elsewhere. It is denoted by I_n, or simply by I if the size is immaterial or can be trivially determined by the context. (In some fields, such as quantum mechanics, the _____ is denoted by a boldface one, 1; otherwise it is identical to I.)
   a. Identity matrix
   b. Associativity
   c. Orthogonal
   d. Artinian ideal

10. In linear algebra, a _____ matrix is a square matrix A whose transpose is also its negative; that is, it satisfies the equation:

$$A^T = -A$$

or in component form, if $A = (a_{ij})$:

$$a_{ij} = -a_{ji} \text{ for all i and j.}$$

For example, the following matrix is _____:

$$\begin{bmatrix} 0 & 2 & -1 \\ -2 & 0 & -4 \\ 1 & 4 & 0 \end{bmatrix}.$$

Compare this with a symmetric matrix whose transpose is the same as the matrix

$$A^T = A,$$

or to an orthogonal matrix, the transpose of which is equal to its inverse:

$$A^T = A^{-1}.$$

Sums and scalar products of _____ matrices are again _____. Hence, the _____ matrices form a vector space. Its dimension is $\frac{n(n-1)}{2}$.

a. Complex Hadamard matrix
c. Skew-symmetric

b. Bisymmetric matrix
d. Duplication matrix

11. In linear algebra, a _____ is a square matrix with entries being the unit fractions

$$H_{ij} = \frac{1}{i+j-1}.$$

For example, this is the 5 × 5 _____:

$$H = \begin{bmatrix} 1 & \frac{1}{2} & \frac{1}{3} & \frac{1}{4} & \frac{1}{5} \\ \frac{1}{2} & \frac{1}{3} & \frac{1}{4} & \frac{1}{5} & \frac{1}{6} \\ \frac{1}{3} & \frac{1}{4} & \frac{1}{5} & \frac{1}{6} & \frac{1}{7} \\ \frac{1}{4} & \frac{1}{5} & \frac{1}{6} & \frac{1}{7} & \frac{1}{8} \\ \frac{1}{5} & \frac{1}{6} & \frac{1}{7} & \frac{1}{8} & \frac{1}{9} \end{bmatrix}.$$

The _____ can be regarded as derived from the integral

$$H_{ij} = \int_0^1 x^{i+j-2}\, dx,$$

that is, as a Gramian matrix for powers of x. It arises in the least squares approximation of arbitrary functions by polynomials.

The Hilbert matrices are canonical examples of ill-conditioned matrices, making them notoriously difficult to use in numerical computation.

a. Triangular matrix
c. Diagonally dominant
b. Hilbert matrix
d. Minimum degree algorithm

12. In linear algebra, a _____ matrix is a matrix that is 'almost' a diagonal matrix. To be exact: a _____ matrix has nonzero elements only in the main diagonal, the first diagonal below this, and the first diagonal above the main diagonal.

For example, the following matrix is _____:

$$\begin{pmatrix} 1 & 4 & 0 & 0 \\ 3 & 4 & 1 & 0 \\ 0 & 2 & 3 & 4 \\ 0 & 0 & 1 & 3 \end{pmatrix}.$$

A determinant formed from a _____ matrix is known as a continuant.

a. -equivalence
c. -module
b. 2-bridge knot
d. Tridiagonal

13. In linear algebra, a _____ is a matrix that is 'almost' a diagonal matrix. To be exact: a _____ has nonzero elements only in the main diagonal, the first diagonal below this, and the first diagonal above the main diagonal.

For example, the following matrix is tridiagonal:

$$\begin{pmatrix} 1 & 4 & 0 & 0 \\ 3 & 4 & 1 & 0 \\ 0 & 2 & 3 & 4 \\ 0 & 0 & 1 & 3 \end{pmatrix}.$$

A determinant formed from a _____ is known as a continuant.

a. Similar
b. Diagonalizable matrix
c. Tridiagonal matrix
d. Wilkinson matrices

14. In mathematics, a _____ is a matrix formed by selecting certain rows and columns from a bigger matrix. That is, as an array, it is cut down to those entries constrained by row and column.

For example

$$\mathbf{A} = \begin{bmatrix} a_{11} & a_{12} & a_{13} & a_{14} \\ a_{21} & a_{22} & a_{23} & a_{24} \\ a_{31} & a_{32} & a_{33} & a_{34} \end{bmatrix}.$$

Then

$$\mathbf{A}[1,2;1,3,4] = \begin{bmatrix} a_{11} & a_{13} & a_{14} \\ a_{21} & a_{23} & a_{24} \end{bmatrix}$$

is a _____ of A formed by rows 1,2 and columns 1,3,4.

a. Quasideterminant
b. Lie product formula
c. Submatrix
d. Smith normal form

15. In several fields of mathematics the term _____ is used with different but closely related meanings. They all relate to the notion of mapping the elements of a set to other elements of the same set, i.e., exchanging (or 'permuting') elements of a set.

The general concept of _____ can be defined more formally in different contexts:

In combinatorics, a _____ is usually understood to be a sequence containing each element from a finite set once, and only once.

a. Permutation
b. Binary function
c. Rupture field
d. Near-field

16. In linear algebra, the _____ describes a particular construction that is useful for calculating both the determinant and inverse of square matrices. Specifically the _____ of the (i, j) entry of a matrix, also known as the (i, j) _____ of that matrix, is the signed minor of that entry.

Finding the minors of a matrix A is a multi-step process:

1. Choose an entry a_{ij} from the matrix.
2. Cross out the entries that lie in the corresponding row i and column j.
3. Rewrite the matrix without the marked entries.
4. Obtain the determinant M_{ij} of this new matrix.

M_{ij} is termed the minor for entry a_{ij}.

If i + j is an even number, the _____ C_{ij} of a_{ij} coincides with its minor:

$$C_{ij} = M_{ij}.$$

Otherwise, it is equal to the additive inverse of its minor:

$$C_{ij} = -M_{ij}.$$

If A is a square matrix, then the minor of its entry a_{ij}, also known as the i,j, or (i,j), or (i,j)[th] minor of A, is denoted by M_{ij} and is defined to be the determinant of the submatrix obtained by removing from A its i-th row and j-th column.

a. Complex structure
b. Cofactor
c. Coefficient matrix
d. Resolvent set

17. In linear algebra, a _____ is one that is 'almost' triangular. To be exact, an upper _____ has zero entries below the first subdiagonal, and a lower _____ has zero entries above the first superdiagonal. They are named for Karl Hessenberg.

a. Duplication matrix
b. Main diagonal
c. Paley construction
d. Hessenberg matrix

18. In mathematics, in matrix theory, a _____ is a square (0,1)-matrix that has exactly one entry 1 in each row and each column and 0's elsewhere. Each such matrix represents a specific permutation of m elements and, when used to multiply another matrix, can produce that permutation in the rows or columns of the other matrix.

Given a permutation π of m elements,

$$\pi : \{1, \ldots, m\} \to \{1, \ldots, m\}$$

Chapter 5. Determinants

given in two-line form by

$$\begin{pmatrix} 1 & 2 & \cdots & m \\ \pi(1) & \pi(2) & \cdots & \pi(m) \end{pmatrix},$$

its _____ is the m × m matrix P_π whose entries are all 0 except that in row i, the entry π(i) equals 1.

a. Permutation matrix
c. Main diagonal
b. Skew-symmetric
d. Hessenberg matrix

19. In linear algebra, the _____ of a matrix A is another matrix A^T (also written A', A^{tr} or ^tA) created by any one of the following equivalent actions:

- write the rows of A as the columns of A^T
- write the columns of A as the rows of A^T
- reflect A by its main diagonal (which starts from the top left) to obtain A^T

Formally, the _____ of an m × n matrix A with elements A_{ij} is the n × m matrix

$$A^T_{ij} = A_{ji} \text{ for } 1 \leq i \leq n, 1 \leq j \leq m.$$

The _____ of a scalar is the same scalar.

- $\begin{bmatrix} 1 & 2 \end{bmatrix}^T = \begin{bmatrix} 1 \\ 2 \end{bmatrix}.$

- $\begin{bmatrix} 1 & 2 \\ 3 & 4 \end{bmatrix}^T = \begin{bmatrix} 1 & 3 \\ 2 & 4 \end{bmatrix}.$

- $\begin{bmatrix} 1 & 2 \\ 3 & 4 \\ 5 & 6 \end{bmatrix}^T = \begin{bmatrix} 1 & 3 & 5 \\ 2 & 4 & 6 \end{bmatrix}.$

For matrices A, B and scalar c we have the following properties of _____:

1. $\left(\mathbf{A}^T\right)^T = \mathbf{A}$

Chapter 5. Determinants

Taking the _____ is an involution (self inverse.)

- $(\mathbf{A}+\mathbf{B})^{\mathrm{T}} = \mathbf{A}^{\mathrm{T}} + \mathbf{B}^{\mathrm{T}}$

    The _____ respects addition.

- $(\mathbf{AB})^{\mathrm{T}} = \mathbf{B}^{\mathrm{T}}\mathbf{A}^{\mathrm{T}}$

    Note that the order of the factors reverses. From this one can deduce that a square matrix A is invertible if and only if A^T is invertible, and in this case we have $(A^{-1})^T = (A^T)^{-1}$. It is relatively easy to extend this result to the general case of multiple matrices, where we find that $(ABC...XYZ)^T = Z^T Y^T X^T...C^T B^T A^T$.

- $(c\mathbf{A})^{\mathrm{T}} = c\mathbf{A}^{\mathrm{T}}$

    The _____ of a scalar is the same scalar. Together with (2), this states that the _____ is a linear map from the space of m × n matrices to the space of all n × m matrices.

- $\det(\mathbf{A}^{\mathrm{T}}) = \det(\mathbf{A})$

    The determinant of a square matrix is the same as that of its _____.

- The dot product of two column vectors a and b can be computed as

$$\mathbf{a} \cdot \mathbf{b} = \mathbf{a}^{\mathrm{T}}\mathbf{b},$$

which is written as $a_i b^i$ in Einstein notation.
- If A has only real entries, then $A^T A$ is a positive-semidefinite matrix.

- $(\mathbf{A}^{\mathrm{T}})^{-1} = (\mathbf{A}^{-1})^{\mathrm{T}}$

    The _____ of an invertible matrix is also invertible, and its inverse is the _____ of the inverse of the original matrix.

- If A is a square matrix, then its eigenvalues are equal to the eigenvalues of its _____.

A square matrix whose _____ is equal to itself is called a symmetric matrix; that is, A is symmetric if

$$\mathbf{A}^{\mathrm{T}} = \mathbf{A}.$$

Chapter 5. Determinants

A square matrix whose _____ is also its inverse is called an orthogonal matrix; that is, G is orthogonal if

$$GG^T = G^TG = I_n,$$ the identity matrix, i.e. $G^T = G^{-1}$.

A square matrix whose _____ is equal to its negative is called skew-symmetric matrix; that is, A is skew-symmetric if

$$A^T = -A.$$

The conjugate _____ of the complex matrix A, written as A*, is obtained by taking the _____ of A and the complex conjugate of each entry:

$$A^* = (\overline{A})^T = \overline{(A^T)}.$$

If f: V→W is a linear map between vector spaces V and W with nondegenerate bilinear forms, we define the _____ of f to be the linear map ^tf: W→V, determined by

$$B_V(v, {}^tf(w)) = B_W(f(v), w) \quad \forall \ v \in V, w \in W.$$

Here, B_V and B_W are the bilinear forms on V and W respectively. The matrix of the _____ of a map is the transposed matrix only if the bases are orthonormal with respect to their bilinear forms.

Over a complex vector space, one often works with sesquilinear forms instead of bilinear (conjugate-linear in one argument.)

a. Tridiagonal matrix
c. Drazin inverse
b. Levinson recursion
d. Transpose

20. In mathematics and group theory, a _____ system for the action of a group G on a set X is a partition of X that is G-invariant. In terms of the associated equivalence relation on X, G-invariance means that

        x ≡ y implies gx ≡ gy

for all g in G and all x, y in X. The action of G on X determines a natural action of G on any _____ system for X.

Each element of the _____ system is called a _____.

a. Frobenius group
c. Parker vector
b. Symmetric group
d. Block

Chapter 5. Determinants

21. In the mathematical discipline of matrix theory, a _____ or a partitioned matrix is a partition of a matrix into rectangular smaller matrices called blocks. Looking at it another way, the matrix is written in terms of smaller matrices written side-by-side. A _____ must conform to a consistent way of splitting up the rows, and the columns: we group the rows into some adjacent 'bunches', and the columns likewise.
    a. Symplectic matrix
    b. Vandermonde matrix
    c. Bidiagonal matrix
    d. Block matrix

22. In linear algebra and the theory of matrices, the _____ of a matrix block (i.e., a submatrix within a larger matrix) is defined as follows. Suppose A, B, C, D are respectively p×p, p×q, q×p and q×q matrices, and D is invertible. Let

$$M = \begin{bmatrix} A & B \\ C & D \end{bmatrix}$$

so that M is a (p+q)×(p+q) matrix.

    a. Homogeneous function
    b. Fundamental theorem of linear algebra
    c. Schur complement
    d. Projection-valued measure

23. In discrete mathematics and predominantly in set theory, a _____ is a concept used in comparisons of sets to refer to the unique values of one set in relation to another. The terms 'absolute' and 'relative' _____ refer to more specific applications of the concept, with universal complements referring to elements unique to the universal set and the latter referring to the unique elements of one set in relation to another. In this image, the universal set is represented by the border of the image, and the set A as a disc.
    a. -module
    b. Pointed set
    c. Complement
    d. -equivalence

24. In mathematics, particularly matrix theory and combinatorics, the _____ is an infinite matrix containing the binomial coefficients as its elements. There are 3 ways this can be achieved - either as an upper-triangular matrix, a lower-triangular matrix, or as a symmetric matrix. The 5×5 truncations of these are shown below.
    a. Conference matrix
    b. Butson-type
    c. Polynomial matrix
    d. Pascal matrix

25. A _____ is one of the basic shapes of geometry: a polygon with three corners or vertices and three sides or edges which are line segments. A _____ with vertices A, B, and C is denoted ABC.

In Euclidean geometry any three non-collinear points determine a unique _____ and a unique plane (i.e. a two-dimensional Euclidean space.)

    a. Triangle
    b. 2-bridge knot
    c. -equivalence
    d. -module

26. In geometry, a _____ is a quadrilateral with two sets of parallel sides. The opposite or facing sides of a _____ are of equal length, and the opposite angles of a _____ are of equal size. The three-dimensional counterpart of a _____ is a parallelepiped.

Chapter 5. Determinants

a. Parallelogram
b. -equivalence
c. 2-bridge knot
d. -module

27. In vector calculus, the _____ is shorthand for either the _____ matrix or its determinant, the _____ determinant.

In algebraic geometry the _____ of a curve means the _____ variety: a group variety associated to the curve, in which the curve can be embedded.

These concepts are all named after the mathematician Carl Gustav Jacob Jacobi.

a. Hessian matrix
b. Critical point
c. Laplace operator
d. Jacobian

28. In vector calculus, the Jacobian is shorthand for either the _____ or its determinant, the Jacobian determinant.

In algebraic geometry the Jacobian of a curve means the Jacobian variety: a group variety associated to the curve, in which the curve can be embedded.

These concepts are all named after the mathematician Carl Gustav Jacob Jacobi.

a. -equivalence
b. 2-bridge knot
c. -module
d. Jacobian matrix

29. In mathematics and physics, the _____ is a common mnemonic for understanding notation conventions for vectors in 3 dimensions. It was invented for use in electromagnetism by British physicist Zachariah William Cole in the late 1800s.

When choosing three vectors that must be at right angles to each other, there are two distinct solutions, so when expressing this idea in mathematics, one must remove the ambiguity of which solution is meant.

a. 2-bridge knot
b. -equivalence
c. -module
d. Right-hand rule

30. In mathematics, the _____ is a binary operation on two vectors in a three-dimensional Euclidean space that results in another vector which is perpendicular to the plane containing the two input vectors. The algebra defined by the _____ is neither commutative nor associative. It contrasts with the dot product which produces a scalar result.

a. Cross product
b. Formal power series
c. Differential graded algebra
d. Row space

31. In vector calculus, there are two ways of multiplying three vectors together, to make a _____ of vectors. Three vectors defining a parallelepiped

The scalar _____ is defined as the dot product of one of the vectors with the cross product of the other two.

Chapter 5. Determinants

Geometrically, the scalar _____

$$\mathbf{a} \cdot (\mathbf{b} \times \mathbf{c})$$

is the (signed) volume of the parallelepiped defined by the three vectors given.

a. 2-bridge knot
c. -equivalence

b. -module
d. Triple product

32. In mathematics, a _____ is a square matrix whose entries are either +1 or −1 and whose rows are mutually orthogonal. In geometric terms, this means that every two different rows in a _____ represent two perpendicular vectors, while in combinatorial terms, it means that every two different rows have matching entries in exactly half of their columns and mismatched entries in the remaining columns. It is a consequence of this definition that the corresponding properties hold for columns as well as rows.

a. 2-bridge knot
c. -equivalence

b. Hadamard matrix
d. -module

Chapter 6. Eigenvalues and Eigenvectors

1. For each eigenvector of a linear transformation, there is a corresponding scalar value called an _____ for that vector, which determines the amount the eigenvector is scaled under the linear transformation. For example, an _____ of +2 means that the eigenvector is doubled in length and points in the same direction. An _____ of +1 means that the eigenvector is unchanged, while an _____ of −1 means that the eigenvector is reversed in sense.
    a. AKS primality test
    b. ADE classification
    c. Abelian P-root group
    d. Eigenvalue

2. For each _____ of a linear transformation, there is a corresponding scalar value called an eigenvalue for that vector, which determines the amount the _____ is scaled under the linear transformation. For example, an eigenvalue of +2 means that the _____ is doubled in length and points in the same direction. An eigenvalue of +1 means that the _____ is unchanged, while an eigenvalue of −1 means that the _____ is reversed in sense.
    a. ADE classification
    b. Abelian P-root group
    c. AKS primality test
    d. Eigenvector

3. In mathematics, a _____ is a rectangular array of numbers. This way, matrices can record data that depend on multiple parameters. In particular they are used to keep track of the coefficients of multiple linear equations. Matrices are closely connected to linear transformations, which are higher-dimensional analogs of linear functions, i.e., functions of the form f(x) = c · x, where c is a constant. This map corresponds to a _____ with one row and column, with entry c. In addition to a number of elementary, entrywise operations such as _____ addition a key notion is _____ multiplication, which displays a number of features not encountered in numbers; for example, products of matrices depend on the order of the factors, unlike products of real numbers, say, where c · d = d · c for any two numbers c and d.
    a. Heap
    b. Commutativity
    c. Matrix
    d. Polynomial expression

4. In linear algebra and functional analysis, a _____ is a linear transformation P from a vector space to itself such that $P^2 = P$. It leaves its image unchanged. Though abstract, this definition of '_____' formalizes and generalizes the idea of graphical _____.
    a. Convolution power
    b. Lumer-Phillips theorem
    c. C_0-semigroup
    d. Projection

5. In linear algebra, a _____ matrix is a matrix that is 'almost' a diagonal matrix. To be exact: a _____ matrix has nonzero elements only in the main diagonal, the first diagonal below this, and the first diagonal above the main diagonal.

    For example, the following matrix is _____:

    $$\begin{pmatrix} 1 & 4 & 0 & 0 \\ 3 & 4 & 1 & 0 \\ 0 & 2 & 3 & 4 \\ 0 & 0 & 1 & 3 \end{pmatrix}.$$

    A determinant formed from a _____ matrix is known as a continuant.

    a. -equivalence
    b. 2-bridge knot
    c. -module
    d. Tridiagonal

Chapter 6. Eigenvalues and Eigenvectors

6. In linear algebra, a _____ is a linear transformation that squares to the identity (R² = I, where R is in K dimensional space), also known as an involution in the general linear group. In addition to reflections across hyperplanes, the class of general reflections includes point reflections, reflections across subspaces of intermediate dimension, and non-orthogonal reflections.

A _____ over a hyperplane in an inner product space is necessarily symmetric, but a general _____ need not be as the example $\begin{bmatrix} 1 & 0 \\ 1 & -1 \end{bmatrix}$ shows.

a. Morphism
c. Reflection
b. Homomorphic secret sharing
d. Shear mappings

7. In mathematics, the _____ of a ring R, often denoted char(R), is defined to be the smallest number of times one must add the ring's multiplicative identity element (1) to itself to get the additive identity element (0); the ring is said to have _____ zero if this repeated sum never reaches the additive identity. That is, char(R) is the smallest positive number n such that

$$\underbrace{1 + \cdots + 1}_{n \text{ summands}} = 0$$

if such a number n exists, and 0 otherwise. The _____ may also be taken to be the exponent of the ring's additive group, that is, the smallest positive n such that

$$\underbrace{a + \cdots + a}_{n \text{ summands}} = 0$$

for every element a of the ring (again, if n exists; otherwise zero.)

a. Characteristic
c. Coherent ring
b. Hereditary
d. Free ideal ring

8. In discrete mathematics, the _____ is used when solving recurrence problems. One can specify a recurrence relation of the form

$$t_n = At_{n-1} + Bt_{n-2}$$

where the value of t_n is dependent on the values of t_{n-1} and t_{n-2}. When solving a recurrence relation, the goal is to eliminate this dependency and derive an equation of the form

$$t_n = c_1 r_1^n + c_2 r_2^n,$$

where c_1 and c_2 are constants and r_1 and r_2 are the roots of the _____

$$r^2 - Ar - B = 0,$$

where A and B are the constants defined in the original recurrence relation.

a. -equivalence
b. -module
c. Characteristic equation
d. 2-bridge knot

9. Economics is the social science that studies the production, distribution, and consumption of goods and services. The term economics comes from the Ancient Greek oá¼°κονομῖα from oá¼¶κος (oikos, 'house') + vĩŒµος (nomos, 'custom' or 'law'), hence 'rules of the house(hold)'. Current _____ models developed out of the broader field of political economy in the late 19th century, owing to a desire to use an empirical approach more akin to the physical sciences.

a. Abelian P-root group
b. AKS primality test
c. Economic
d. ADE classification

10. where B is the _____ of the product. To remove A_1 from the product, we can then write

$$\mathbf{A}_1^{-1}(\mathbf{A}_1\mathbf{A}_2 \cdots \mathbf{A}_n)\mathbf{B} = \mathbf{A}_1^{-1}\mathbf{I}$$

which would reduce the equation to

$$(\mathbf{A}_2\mathbf{A}_3 \cdots \mathbf{A}_n)\mathbf{B} = \mathbf{A}_1^{-1}\mathbf{I}.$$

Likewise, then, from

$$\mathbf{A}_2^{-1}(\mathbf{A}_2\mathbf{A}_3 \cdots \mathbf{A}_n)\mathbf{B} = \mathbf{A}_2^{-1}\mathbf{A}_1^{-1}\mathbf{I}$$

which simplifies to

$$(\mathbf{A}_3\mathbf{A}_4 \cdots \mathbf{A}_n)\mathbf{B} = \mathbf{A}_2^{-1}\mathbf{A}_1^{-1}\mathbf{I}.$$

If one repeat the process up to A_n, the equation becomes

$$\mathbf{B} = \mathbf{A}_n^{-1}\mathbf{A}_{n-1}^{-1} \cdots \mathbf{A}_2^{-1}\mathbf{A}_1^{-1}\mathbf{I}$$

$$\mathbf{B} = \mathbf{A}_n^{-1}\mathbf{A}_{n-1}^{-1} \cdots \mathbf{A}_2^{-1}\mathbf{A}_1^{-1}$$

but B is the _____, i.e. $\mathbf{B} = (\mathbf{A}_1\mathbf{A}_2 \cdots \mathbf{A}_n)^{-1}$ so the property is established.

Chapter 6. Eigenvalues and Eigenvectors

Over the field of real numbers, the set of singular n-by-n matrices, considered as a subset of $R^{n \times n}$, is a null set, i.e., has Lebesgue measure zero.

a. ADE classification
b. Abelian P-root group
c. Inverse matrix
d. AKS primality test

11. In linear algebra, the _____ of an n-by-n square matrix A is defined to be the sum of the elements on the main diagonal (the diagonal from the upper left to the lower right) of A, i.e.,

$$\operatorname{tr}(A) = a_{11} + a_{22} + \cdots + a_{nn} = \sum_{i=1}^{n} a_{ii}$$

where a_{ij} represents the entry on the ith row and jth column of A. Equivalently, the _____ of a matrix is the sum of its eigenvalues, making it an invariant with respect to a change of basis. This characterization can be used to define the _____ for a linear operator in general.

Note that the _____ is only defined for a square matrix (i.e. n×n.)

a. Defective matrix
b. Dot product
c. Trace
d. Coefficient matrix

12. In mathematics, an _____ is a complex number whose squared value is a real number less than or equal to zero. The imaginary unit, denoted by i or j, is an example of an _____. If y is a real number, then i·y is an _____, because:

$$(i \cdot y)^2 = i^2 \cdot y^2 = -y^2 \leq 0.$$

Imaginary numbers were defined in 1572 by Rafael Bombelli.

a. ADE classification
b. AKS primality test
c. Abelian P-root group
d. Imaginary number

13. In mathematics, two vectors are _____ if they are perpendicular, i.e., they form a right angle. The word comes from the Greek á½€ρθÏŒς , meaning 'straight', and γωνῖα (gonia), meaning 'angle'. For example, a subway and the street above, although they do not physically intersect, are _____ if they cross at a right angle.

a. Orthogonal
b. Unital
c. Embedding
d. Expression

14. In linear algebra, an _____ is a square matrix with real entries whose columns (or rows) are orthogonal unit vectors (i.e., orthonormal.) Equivalently, a matrix Q is orthogonal if its transpose is equal to its inverse:

$$Q^T Q = QQ^T = I.$$

As a linear transformation, an _____ preserves the dot product of vectors, and therefore acts as an isometry of Euclidean space, such as a rotation or reflection.

The set of n × n orthogonal matrices forms a group O(n), known as the orthogonal group.

a. Unimodular matrix
c. Alternating sign matrix
b. Orthogonal matrix
d. Unistochastic matrix

15. In geometry, two lines or planes (or a line and a plane), are considered _____ to each other if they form congruent adjacent angles (an L-shape.) The term may be used as a noun or adjective. Thus, referring to Figure 1, the line AB is the _____ to CD through the point B. Note that by definition, a line is infinitely long, and strictly speaking AB and CD in this example represent line segments of two infinitely long lines.

a. -equivalence
c. -module
b. 2-bridge knot
d. Perpendicular

16. In geometry and linear algebra, a _____ is a transformation in a plane or in space that describes the motion of a rigid body around a fixed point. A _____ is different from a translation, which has no fixed points, and from a reflection, which 'flips' the bodies it is transforming. A _____ and the above-mentioned transformations are isometries; they leave the distance between any two points unchanged after the transformation.

a. Shear mappings
c. Rotation
b. Real matrices
d. Reflection

17. In linear algebra, a _____ is any matrix that acts as a rotation of Euclidean space. For example, the matrix

$$\begin{bmatrix} \cos\theta & -\sin\theta \\ \sin\theta & \cos\theta \end{bmatrix}$$

rotates vectors in the plane counterclockwise by an angle of θ. In three dimensions, rotation matrices are among the simplest algebraic descriptions of rotations, and are used extensively for computations in geometry, physics, and computer graphics.

a. Rotational symmetry
c. 9-j symbols
b. Spin magnetic moment
d. Rotation matrix

18. In linear algebra, a _____ matrix is a square matrix A whose transpose is also its negative; that is, it satisfies the equation:

$$A^T = -A$$

or in component form, if A = (a_{ij}) :

a_{ij} = − a_{ji} for all i and j.

For example, the following matrix is _____ :

$$\begin{bmatrix} 0 & 2 & -1 \\ -2 & 0 & -4 \\ 1 & 4 & 0 \end{bmatrix}.$$

Compare this with a symmetric matrix whose transpose is the same as the matrix

$$A^T = A,$$

or to an orthogonal matrix, the transpose of which is equal to its inverse:

$$A^T = A^{-1}.$$

Sums and scalar products of _____ matrices are again _____. Hence, the _____ matrices form a vector space. Its dimension is $\frac{n(n-1)}{2}$.

a. Duplication matrix
c. Bisymmetric matrix
b. Complex Hadamard matrix
d. Skew-symmetric

19. In mathematics, an _____ is the finite or bounded case of a conic section, the geometric shape that results from cutting a circular conical or cylindrical surface with an oblique plane . It is also the locus of all points of the plane whose distances to two fixed points add to the same constant.

Ellipses also arise as images of a circle or a sphere under parallel projection, and some cases of perspective projection.

a. Ellipse
c. ADE classification
b. AKS primality test
d. Abelian P-root group

20. In linear algebra, two n-by-n matrices A and B are called _____ if

$$B = P^{-1}AP$$

for some invertible n-by-n matrix P. _____ matrices represent the same linear transformation under two different bases, with P being the change of basis matrix.

The matrix P is sometimes called a similarity transformation. In the context of matrix groups, similarity is sometimes referred to as conjugacy, with _____ matrices being conjugate.

a. Similar
b. Zero matrix
c. Cartan matrix
d. Skew-symmetric

21. In geometry, a _____ is a quadrilateral with two sets of parallel sides. The opposite or facing sides of a _____ are of equal length, and the opposite angles of a _____ are of equal size. The three-dimensional counterpart of a _____ is a parallelepiped.

a. -equivalence
b. 2-bridge knot
c. -module
d. Parallelogram

22. In several fields of mathematics the term _____ is used with different but closely related meanings. They all relate to the notion of mapping the elements of a set to other elements of the same set, i.e., exchanging (or 'permuting') elements of a set.

The general concept of _____ can be defined more formally in different contexts:

In combinatorics, a _____ is usually understood to be a sequence containing each element from a finite set once, and only once.

a. Near-field
b. Rupture field
c. Permutation
d. Binary function

23. In mathematics, in matrix theory, a _____ is a square (0,1)-matrix that has exactly one entry 1 in each row and each column and 0's elsewhere. Each such matrix represents a specific permutation of m elements and, when used to multiply another matrix, can produce that permutation in the rows or columns of the other matrix.

Given a permutation π of m elements,

$$\pi : \{1, \ldots, m\} \to \{1, \ldots, m\}$$

given in two-line form by

$$\begin{pmatrix} 1 & 2 & \cdots & m \\ \pi(1) & \pi(2) & \cdots & \pi(m) \end{pmatrix},$$

its _____ is the m × m matrix P_π whose entries are all 0 except that in row i, the entry π(i) equals 1.

a. Permutation matrix
b. Hessenberg matrix
c. Main diagonal
d. Skew-symmetric

Chapter 6. Eigenvalues and Eigenvectors

24. A _____ is a three-dimensional solid object bounded by six square faces, facets or sides, with three meeting at each vertex. The _____ can also be called a regular hexahedron and is one of the five Platonic solids. It is a special kind of square prism, of rectangular parallelepiped and of trigonal trapezohedron.
   a. -module
   b. 2-bridge knot
   c. -equivalence
   d. Cube

25. In geometry, a _____ is an n-dimensional analogue of a square (n = 2) and a cube (n = 3.) It is a closed, compact, convex figure whose 1-skeleton consists of groups of opposite parallel line segments aligned in each of the space's dimensions, at right angles to each other and of the same length.

An n-dimensional _____ is also called an n-cube.

   a. 2-bridge knot
   b. Hypercube
   c. -equivalence
   d. -module

26. In algebra, a _____ is a function depending on n that associates a scalar, det(A), to an n×n square matrix A. The fundamental geometric meaning of a _____ is a scale factor for measure when A is regarded as a linear transformation. Determinants are important both in calculus, where they enter the substitution rule for several variables, and in multilinear algebra.

For a fixed nonnegative integer n, there is a unique _____ function for the n×n matrices over any commutative ring R. In particular, this function exists when R is the field of real or complex numbers.

   a. Leibniz formula
   b. Functional determinant
   c. Determinant
   d. Pfaffian

27. In quantum physics, the _____ states that certain physical quantities, like position and momentum, cannot both have precise values at the same time. The narrower the probability distribution for one, the wider it is for the other.

In quantum mechanics, a particle is described by a wave.

   a. 2-bridge knot
   b. -module
   c. -equivalence
   d. Heisenberg uncertainty principle

28. A _____ is a specific type of recurrence relation.

An example of a recurrence relation is the logistic map:

$$x_{n+1} = r x_n (1 - x_n)$$

Some simply defined recurrence relations can have very complex (chaotic) behaviours and are sometimes studied by physicists and mathematicians in a field of mathematics known as nonlinear analysis.

Solving a recurrence relation means obtaining a closed-form solution: a non-recursive function of n.

Chapter 6. Eigenvalues and Eigenvectors

a. -equivalence
b. -module
c. 2-bridge knot
d. Difference equation

29. The Lucas numbers are an integer sequence named after the mathematician François Édouard Anatole Lucas (1842-1891), who studied both that sequence and the closely related Fibonacci numbers (both are Lucas sequences.) Like the Fibonacci numbers, each _____ is defined to be the sum of its two immediate previous terms, i.e. it is a Fibonacci integer sequence. Consequently, the ratio between two consecutive Lucas numbers converges to the golden ratio.

a. Lucas number
b. -equivalence
c. 2-bridge knot
d. -module

30. In mathematics, a _____ in a (unital) ring R is an invertible element of R, i.e. an element u such that there is a v in R with

$$uv = vu = 1_R,$$ where 1_R is the multiplicative identity element.

That is, u is an invertible element of the multiplicative monoid of R. If $0 \neq 1$ in the ring, then 0 is not a _____.

Unfortunately, the term _____ is also used to refer to the identity element 1_R of the ring, in expressions like ring with a _____ or _____ ring, and also e.g. '_____' matrix.

a. Ascending chain condition on principal ideals
b. Ore extension
c. Ore condition
d. Unit

31. In mathematics, a _____ is a circle with a unit radius, i.e., a circle whose radius is 1. Frequently, especially in trigonometry, 'the' _____ is the circle of radius 1 centered at the origin (0, 0) in the Cartesian coordinate system in the Euclidean plane. The _____ is often denoted S^1; the generalization to higher dimensions is the unit sphere.

a. Unit circle
b. AKS primality test
c. Abelian P-root group
d. ADE classification

32. A _____ is a mathematical equation for an unknown function of one or several variables that relates the values of the function itself and its derivatives of various orders. Differential equations play a prominent role in engineering, physics, economics and other disciplines. Visualization of airflow into a duct modelled using the Navier-Stokes equations, a set of partial differential equations.

Differential equations arise in many areas of science and technology; whenever a deterministic relationship involving some continuously changing quantities (modeled by functions) and their rates of change (expressed as derivatives) is known or postulated.

a. 2-bridge knot
b. -module
c. -equivalence
d. Differential equation

33. In mathematics, the _____ is a matrix function on square matrices analogous to the ordinary exponential function. Abstractly, the _____ gives the connection between a matrix Lie algebra and the corresponding Lie group.

Let X be an n×n real or complex matrix.

a. 2-bridge knot
b. -module
c. -equivalence
d. Matrix exponential

34. In mathematics, a _____ maps a function, $f(x)$, to another function, $f(x + b) - f(x + a)$.

The forward _____

$$\Delta f(x) = f(x+1) - f(x)$$

occurs frequently in the calculus of finite differences, where it plays a role formally similar to that of the derivative, but used in discrete circumstances. Difference equations can often be solved with techniques very similar to those for solving differential equations.

a. -equivalence
b. Difference operator
c. 2-bridge knot
d. -module

35. In linear algebra, a _____ is a square matrix with constant (positive sloping) skew-diagonals, e.g.:

$$\begin{bmatrix} a & b & c & d & e \\ b & c & d & e & f \\ c & d & e & f & g \\ d & e & f & g & h \\ e & f & g & h & i \end{bmatrix}.$$

In mathematical terms:

$$a_{i,j} = a_{i-1,j+1}.$$

The _____ is closely related to the Toeplitz matrix (a _____ is an upside-down Toeplitz matrix.) For a special case of this matrix see Hilbert matrix.

A Hankel operator on a Hilbert space is one whose matrix with respect to an orthonormal basis is an infinite _____ $(a_{i,j})_{i,j \geq 1}$, where $a_{i,j}$ depends only on $i + j$.

a. Hankel matrix
b. Main diagonal
c. Modal matrix
d. Supermatrix

36. _____ is definite, that is, has a real value with the same sign (positive or negative) for all non-zero x. According to that sign, B is called positive definite or _____. If Q takes both positive and negative values, the bilinear form B is called indefinite.

Chapter 6. Eigenvalues and Eigenvectors

  a. -module
  b. 2-bridge knot
  c. -equivalence
  d. Negative definite

37. In linear algebra, a _____ is a (Hermitian) matrix which in many ways is analogous to a positive real number. The notion is closely related to a positive-definite symmetric bilinear form (or a sesquilinear form in the complex case.)

An n × n real symmetric matrix M is positive definite if $z^T Mz > 0$ for all non-zero vectors z with real entries ($z \in R^n$), where z^T denotes the transpose of z.

  a. Positive-definite matrix
  b. 2-bridge knot
  c. -equivalence
  d. -module

38. In mathematics, particularly matrix theory and combinatorics, the _____ is an infinite matrix containing the binomial coefficients as its elements. There are 3 ways this can be achieved - either as an upper-triangular matrix, a lower-triangular matrix, or as a symmetric matrix. The 5×5 truncations of these are shown below.
  a. Polynomial matrix
  b. Pascal matrix
  c. Conference matrix
  d. Butson-type

39. The set of all symmetry operations considered, on all objects in a set X, can be modeled as a group action g : G × X → X, where the image of g in G and x in X is written as gÂ·x. If, for some g, gÂ·x = y then x and y are said to be symmetrical to each other. For each object x, operations g for which gÂ·x = x form a group, the _____ of the object, a subgroup of G. If the _____ of x is the trivial group then x is said to be asymmetric, otherwise symmetric.
  a. 2-bridge knot
  b. -module
  c. -equivalence
  d. Symmetry group

40. In linear algebra, a _____ is a square matrix, A, that is equal to its transpose

$$A = A^T.$$

The entries of a _____ are symmetric with respect to the main diagonal (top left to bottom right.) So if the entries are written as A = (a_{ij}), then

$$a_{ij} = a_{ji}$$

for all indices i and j. The following 3×3 matrix is symmetric:

$$\begin{bmatrix} 1 & 2 & 3 \\ 2 & 4 & -5 \\ 3 & -5 & 6 \end{bmatrix}.$$

A matrix is called skew-symmetric or antisymmetric if its transpose is the same as its negative.

a. Stieltjes matrix
b. Zero matrix
c. Butson-type
d. Symmetric matrix

41. In the mathematical fields of geometry and linear algebra, a principal axis is a certain line in a Euclidean space associated to an ellipsoid or hyperboloid, generalizing the major and minor axes of an ellipse. The _____ states that the principal axes are perpendicular, and gives a constructive procedure for finding them.

Mathematically, the _____ is a generalization of the method of completing the square from elementary algebra.

a. Barycentric coordinates
b. Rank
c. Homogeneous function
d. Principal axis theorem

42. In mathematics, particularly linear algebra and functional analysis, the _____ is any of a number of results about linear operators or about matrices. In broad terms the _____ provides conditions under which an operator or a matrix can be diagonalized (that is, represented as a diagonal matrix in some basis.) This concept of diagonalization is relatively straightforward for operators on finite-dimensional spaces, but requires some modification for operators on infinite-dimensional spaces.

a. Spectral geometry
b. Spectral asymmetry
c. Spectral radius
d. Spectral theorem

43. In mathematics, the (formal) _____ of a complex vector space V is the complex vector space $\overline{V}$ consisting of all formal complex conjugates of elements of V. That is, $\overline{V}$ is a vector space whose elements are in one-to-one correspondence with the elements of V:

$$\overline{V} = \{\overline{v} \mid v \in V\},$$

with the following rules for addition and scalar multiplication:

$$\overline{v} + \overline{w} = \overline{v + w} \quad \text{and} \quad \alpha \overline{v} = \overline{\overline{\alpha} v}.$$

Here v and w are vectors in V, α is a complex number, and $\overline{\alpha}$ denotes the _____ of α.

In the case where V is a linear subspace of $\mathbb{C}^n$, the formal _____ $\overline{V}$ is naturally isomorphic to the actual _____ subspace of V in $\mathbb{C}^n$.

a. Binomial inverse theorem
b. Conjugate transpose
c. Polynomial basis
d. Complex conjugate

44. In algebra, a _____ of an element in a quadratic extension field of a field K is its image under the unique non-identity automorphism of the extended field that fixes K. If the extension is generated by a square root of an element r of K, then the _____ of $a + b\sqrt{r}$ is $a - b\sqrt{r}$ for $a, b \in K$, and in particular in the case of the field C of complex numbers as an extension of the field R of real numbers (where r = − 1), the complex _____ of a + bi is a − bi.

Forming the sum or product of any element of the extension field with its _____ always gives an element of K. This can be used to rewrite a quotient of numbers in the extended field so that the denominator lies in K, by multiplying numerator and denominator by the _____ of the denominator. This process is called rationalization of the denominator, in particular if K is the field Q of rational numbers.

- a. Field arithmetic
- b. Conjugate
- c. Digital root
- d. K-theory

45. In mathematics, the Cauchy-_____ the Cauchy inequality is a useful inequality encountered in many different settings, such as linear algebra applied to vectors, in analysis applied to infinite series and integration of products, and in probability theory, applied to variances and covariances. The general formulation of the Heisenberg uncertainty principle is derived using the Cauchy-_____ in the Hilbert space of pure quantum states.

The inequality for sums was published by , while the corresponding inequality for integrals was first stated by and rediscovered by

- a. Schwarz inequality
- b. 2-bridge knot
- c. -equivalence
- d. -module

46. In mathematics, an _____ is a statement about the relative size or order of two objects, or about whether they are the same or not

- The notation a < b means that a is less than b.
- The notation a > b means that a is greater than b.
- The notation a ≠ b means that a is not equal to b, but does not say that one is bigger than the other or even that they can be compared in size.

In all these cases, a is not equal to b, hence, '_____'.

These relations are known as strict _____

- The notation a ≤ b means that a is less than or equal to b (or, equivalently, not greater than b);
- The notation a ≥ b means that a is greater than or equal to b (or, equivalently, not smaller than b);

An additional use of the notation is to show that one quantity is much greater than another, normally by several orders of magnitude.

- The notation a ≪ b means that a is much less than b.
- The notation a ≫ b means that a is much greater than b.

If the sense of the _____ is the same for all values of the variables for which its members are defined, then the _____ is called an 'absolute' or 'unconditional' _____. If the sense of an _____ holds only for certain values of the variables involved, but is reversed or destroyed for other values of the variables, it is called a conditional _____.

Chapter 6. Eigenvalues and Eigenvectors

One can apply the same algebraic operations to inequalities as one would apply for solving equalities. For example, to find x for the _____ 10x > 20 one would divide 20 by 10 to obtain x > 2.

a. Abelian P-root group
c. AKS primality test
b. ADE classification
d. Inequality

47. In mathematics, the _____ is a specific kind of Fourier transform, used in Fourier analysis. It transforms one function into another, which is called the frequency domain representation, or simply the _____, of the original function (which is often a function in the time domain.) But the _____ requires an input function that is discrete and whose non-zero values have a limited (finite) duration.

a. Modulated complex lapped transform
c. Fourier transform on finite groups
b. Discrete Fourier Transform
d. Multitaper

48. In mathematics, an element x of a ring R is called _____ if there exists some positive integer n such that $x^n = 0$.

The term was introduced by Benjamin Peirce in the context of elements of an algebra that vanish when raised to a power.

- This definition can be applied in particular to square matrices. The matrix

$$A = \begin{pmatrix} 0 & 1 & 0 \\ 0 & 0 & 1 \\ 0 & 0 & 0 \end{pmatrix}$$

is _____ because $A^3 = 0$. See _____ matrix for more.

a. Hochschild homology
c. Product ring
b. Ring of integers
d. Nilpotent

49. A complex square matrix A is a _____ if

$$A^*A = AA^*$$

where A* is the conjugate transpose of A. That is, a matrix is normal if it commutes with its conjugate transpose.

If A is a real matrix, then $A^* = A^T$; it is normal if $A^T A = A A^T$.

Normality is a convenient test for diagonalizability: every _____ can be converted to a diagonal matrix by a unitary transform, and every matrix which can be made diagonal by a unitary transform is also normal, but finding the desired transform requires much more work than simply testing to see whether the matrix is normal.

a. Main diagonal
c. Normal matrix
b. Duplication matrix
d. Hamiltonian matrix

Chapter 6. Eigenvalues and Eigenvectors

50. The _____ of an angle is the ratio of the length of the adjacent side to the length of the hypotenuse. In our case

$$\cos A = \frac{\text{adjacent}}{\text{hypotenuse}} = \frac{b}{h}.$$

The tangent of an angle is the ratio of the length of the opposite side to the length of the adjacent side. In our case

$$\tan A = \frac{\text{opposite}}{\text{adjacent}} = \frac{a}{b}.$$

The remaining three functions are best defined using the above three functions.

a. -module
b. 2-bridge knot
c. Cosine
d. -equivalence

51. In a totally ordered set all elements are mutually comparable, so such a set can have at most one minimal element and at most one maximal element. Then, due to mutual comparability, the minimal element will also be the least element and the maximal element will also be the greatest element. Thus in a totally ordered set we can simply use the terms _____ and maximum.

a. -equivalence
b. Minimum
c. 2-bridge knot
d. -module

52. In mathematics, a _____ is a point in the domain of a function of two variables which is a stationary point but not a local extremum. At such a point, in general, the surface resembles a saddle that curves up in one direction, and curves down in a different direction (like a mountain pass.) In terms of contour lines, a _____ can be recognized, in general, by a contour that appears to intersect itself.

a. Gauss map
b. Weingarten equations
c. Ridge
d. Saddle point

53. Let f be a differentiable function, and let f'(x) be its derivative. The derivative of f'(x) (if it has one) is written f''(x) and is called the _____ of f. Similarly, the derivative of a _____, if it exists, is written f'''(x) and is called the third derivative of f.

a. Second derivative
b. 2-bridge knot
c. -module
d. -equivalence

54. If B(x, x) ≥ 0 for all x, B is said to be positive _____. Negative _____ bilinear forms are defined similarly.

As an example, let V=R², and consider the bilinear form

$$B(x,y) = c_1 x_1 y_1 + c_2 x_2 y_2$$

where x = (x_1, x_2), y = (y_1, y_2), and c_1 and c_2 are constants.

Chapter 6. Eigenvalues and Eigenvectors

a. -module
b. Semidefinite
c. 2-bridge knot
d. -equivalence

55. _____ is a concept that permeates much of inferential statistics and descriptive statistics. More properly, it is 'the sum of the squared deviations'. Mathematically, it is an unscaled, or unadjusted measure of dispersion (also called variability.)
    a. Sum of squares
    b. -equivalence
    c. -module
    d. 2-bridge knot

56. The _____ is often met for the first time as an operation on a single real function of a single real variable. One of the simplest settings for generalizations is to vector valued functions of several variables (most often the domain forms a vector space as well.) This is the field of multivariable calculus.
    a. -module
    b. 2-bridge knot
    c. -equivalence
    d. Derivative

57. In elementary algebra, _____ is a technique for converting a quadratic polynomial of the form

$$ax^2 + bx + c$$

to the form

$$a(\cdots\cdots)^2 + \text{constant}.$$

The expression inside the parenthesis is of the form x − constant. Thus one converts ax² + bx + c to

$$a(x - h)^2 + k$$

and one must find h and k.

_____ is used in

- solving quadratic equations,
- graphing quadratic functions,
- evaluating integrals in calculus,
- finding Laplace transforms.

In mathematics, _____ is considered a basic algebraic operation, and is often applied without remark in any computation involving quadratic polynomials.

There is a simple formula in elementary algebra for computing the square of a binomial:

$$(x + p)^2 = x^2 + 2px + p^2.$$

For example:

$$(x+3)^2 = x^2 + 6x + 9 \quad (p = 3)$$
$$(x-5)^2 = x^2 - 10x + 25 \quad (p = -5).$$

In any perfect square, the number p is always half the coefficient of x, and then the constant term is equal to p^2.

a. Nested radical
b. Content
c. Reduct
d. Completing the square

58. In mathematics, _____ or factoring is the decomposition of an object ' href='/wiki/Matrix_(mathematics)'>matrix) into a product of other objects, or factors, which when multiplied together give the original. For example, the number 15 factors into primes as 3 × 5, and the polynomial x^2 - 4 factors as (x - 2)(x + 2.) In all cases, a product of simpler objects is obtained.
   a. -module
   b. Factorization
   c. -equivalence
   d. 2-bridge knot

59. In linear algebra, a _____ is a square matrix with entries being the unit fractions

$$H_{ij} = \frac{1}{i+j-1}.$$

For example, this is the 5 × 5 _____:

$$H = \begin{bmatrix} 1 & \frac{1}{2} & \frac{1}{3} & \frac{1}{4} & \frac{1}{5} \\ \frac{1}{2} & \frac{1}{3} & \frac{1}{4} & \frac{1}{5} & \frac{1}{6} \\ \frac{1}{3} & \frac{1}{4} & \frac{1}{5} & \frac{1}{6} & \frac{1}{7} \\ \frac{1}{4} & \frac{1}{5} & \frac{1}{6} & \frac{1}{7} & \frac{1}{8} \\ \frac{1}{5} & \frac{1}{6} & \frac{1}{7} & \frac{1}{8} & \frac{1}{9} \end{bmatrix}.$$

The _____ can be regarded as derived from the integral

$$H_{ij} = \int_0^1 x^{i+j-2}\, dx,$$

that is, as a Gramian matrix for powers of x. It arises in the least squares approximation of arbitrary functions by polynomials.

Chapter 6. Eigenvalues and Eigenvectors 73

The Hilbert matrices are canonical examples of ill-conditioned matrices, making them notoriously difficult to use in numerical computation.

a. Minimum degree algorithm
b. Diagonally dominant
c. Triangular matrix
d. Hilbert matrix

60. A _____ is a set G closed under a binary operation · satisfying the following 3 axioms:

- Associativity: For all a, b and c in G, (a · b) · c = a · (b · c.)
- Identity element: There exists an e∈G such that for all a in G, e · a = a · e = a.
- Inverse element: For each a in G, there is an element b in G such that a · b = b · a = e, where e is an identity element.

Basic examples for groups are the integers Z with addition operation, or rational numbers without zero Q{0} with multiplication. More generally, for any ring R, the units in R form a multiplicative _____ Groups include, however, much more general structures than the above.

a. Product of group subsets
b. Nilpotent group
c. Grigorchuk group
d. Group

61. In linear algebra, a basis for a vector space of dimension n is a sequence of n vectors $a_1, ..., a_n$ with the property that every vector in the space can be expressed uniquely as a linear combination of the basis vectors. Since it is often desirable to work with more than one basis for a vector space, it is of fundamental importance in linear algebra to be able to easily transform coordinate-wise representations of vectors and linear transformations taken with respect to one basis to their equivalent representations with respect to another basis. Such a transformation is called a _____.

a. Split-complex number
b. Generalized singular value decomposition
c. Field of values
d. Change of basis

62. In linear algebra, a _____ is a set of vectors that, in a linear combination, can represent every vector in a given vector space or free module, and such that no element of the set can be represented as a linear combination of the others. In other words, a _____ is a linearly independent spanning set.

a. Basis
b. Supergroup
c. Chirality
d. Minor

63. In mathematics, in particular functional analysis, the _____, or s-numbers of a compact operator T acting on a Hilbert space are defined as the eigenvalues of the operator $\sqrt{T^*T}$ (where T* denotes the adjoint of T and the square root is taken in the operator sense.) The _____ are nonnegative real numbers, usually listed in decreasing order $s_1(T), s_2(T), ...$

a. -module
b. Singular values
c. 2-bridge knot
d. -equivalence

64. In linear algebra, the _____ or unit matrix of size n is the n-by-n square matrix with ones on the main diagonal and zeros elsewhere. It is denoted by I_n, or simply by I if the size is immaterial or can be trivially determined by the context. (In some fields, such as quantum mechanics, the _____ is denoted by a boldface one, 1; otherwise it is identical to I.)

Chapter 6. Eigenvalues and Eigenvectors

a. Associativity
b. Artinian ideal
c. Orthogonal
d. Identity matrix

65. In linear algebra, the _____ is an important factorization of a rectangular real or complex matrix, with several applications in signal processing and statistics. Applications which employ the _____ include computing the pseudoinverse, least squares fitting of data, matrix approximation, and determining the rank, range and null space of a matrix.

Suppose M is an m-by-n matrix whose entries come from the field K, which is either the field of real numbers or the field of complex numbers.

a. -equivalence
b. -module
c. 2-bridge knot
d. Singular Value Decomposition

66. In linear algebra, two vectors in an inner product space are _____ if they are orthogonal and both of unit length. A set of vectors form an _____ set if all vectors in the set are mutually orthogonal and all of unit length. An _____ set which forms a basis is called an _____ basis.

a. Orthonormal
b. Overdetermined
c. Invertible matrix
d. Elementary matrix

67. In mathematics, an _____ of an inner product space V (i.e., a vector space with an inner product), is a set of mutually orthogonal vectors of magnitude 1 (unit vectors) that span the space when infinite linear combinations are allowed. (In some contexts, especially in linear algebra, the concept of basis (linear algebra) means a set of vectors that span a space when only finite linear combinations are allowed.) Such an infinite linear combination is an infinite series, and the concept of convergence relied upon is defined in terms of the space's inner product.

a. Overdetermined
b. Eigendecomposition
c. Orientation
d. Orthonormal basis

68. In mathematics, the _____ is an eigenvalue algorithm: given a matrix A, the algorithm will produce a number λ (the eigenvalue) and a nonzero vector v (the eigenvector), such that Av = λv.

The _____ is a very simple algorithm. It does not compute a matrix decomposition, and hence it can be used when A is a very large sparse matrix.

a. -module
b. 2-bridge knot
c. -equivalence
d. Power iteration

69. The column _____ of a matrix A is the maximal number of linearly independent columns of A. Likewise, the row _____ is the maximal number of linearly independent rows of A.

Since the column _____ and the row _____ are always equal, they are simply called the _____ of A. More abstractly, it is the dimension of the image of A. For the proofs, see, e.g., Murase (1960), Andrea ' Wong (1960), Williams ' Cater (1968), Mackiw (1995).) It is commonly denoted by either rk(A) or _____ A.

a. Generalized Pauli matrices
c. Schur complement

b. Split-complex number
d. Rank

70. A _____ is a square matrix with complex entries which is equal to its own conjugate transpose -- that is, the element in the ith row and jth column is equal to the complex conjugate of the element in the jth row and ith column, for all indices i and j:

$$a_{i,j} = \overline{a_{j,i}}.$$

If the conjugate transpose of a matrix A is denoted by $A^\dagger$, then the Hermitian property can be written concisely as

$$A = A^\dagger.$$

For example,

$$\begin{bmatrix} 3 & 2+i \\ 2-i & 1 \end{bmatrix}$$

is a _____.

The entries on the main diagonal (top left to bottom right) of any _____ are necessarily real. A matrix that has only real entries is Hermitian if and only if it is a symmetric matrix, i.e., if it is symmetric with respect to the main diagonal.

a. Symplectic matrix
c. Permutation matrix

b. Hermitian matrix
d. Levinson recursion

Chapter 7. Linear Transformations

1. In the various branches of mathematics that fall under the heading of abstract algebra, the _____ of a homomorphism measures the degree to which the homomorphism fails to be injective. An important special case is the _____ of a matrix, also called the null space.

    The definition of _____ takes various forms in various contexts.

    a. Completing the square
    b. K-theory
    c. Kernel
    d. Monomial basis

2. In mathematics, an _____ is the finite or bounded case of a conic section, the geometric shape that results from cutting a circular conical or cylindrical surface with an oblique plane . It is also the locus of all points of the plane whose distances to two fixed points add to the same constant.

    Ellipses also arise as images of a circle or a sphere under parallel projection, and some cases of perspective projection.

    a. AKS primality test
    b. Abelian P-root group
    c. Ellipse
    d. ADE classification

3. In linear algebra, a basis for a vector space of dimension n is a sequence of n vectors $α_1, ..., α_n$ with the property that every vector in the space can be expressed uniquely as a linear combination of the basis vectors. Since it is often desirable to work with more than one basis for a vector space, it is of fundamental importance in linear algebra to be able to easily transform coordinate-wise representations of vectors and linear transformations taken with respect to one basis to their equivalent representations with respect to another basis. Such a transformation is called a _____.

    a. Field of values
    b. Generalized singular value decomposition
    c. Split-complex number
    d. Change of basis

4. In linear algebra, a _____ is a set of vectors that, in a linear combination, can represent every vector in a given vector space or free module, and such that no element of the set can be represented as a linear combination of the others. In other words, a _____ is a linearly independent spanning set.

    a. Supergroup
    b. Minor
    c. Chirality
    d. Basis

5. In mathematics, a _____ is a rectangular array of numbers. This way, matrices can record data that depend on multiple parameters. In particular they are used to keep track of the coefficients of multiple linear equations. Matrices are closely connected to linear transformations, which are higher-dimensional analogs of linear functions, i.e., functions of the form f(x) = c · x, where c is a constant. This map corresponds to a _____ with one row and column, with entry c. In addition to a number of elementary, entrywise operations such as _____ addition a key notion is _____ multiplication, which displays a number of features not encountered in numbers; for example, products of matrices depend on the order of the factors, unlike products of real numbers, say, where c · d = d · c for any two numbers c and d.

    a. Polynomial expression
    b. Commutativity
    c. Heap
    d. Matrix

6. In mathematics, especially in the area of abstract algebra known as ring theory, a _____ is a ring with 0 ≠ 1 such that ab = 0 implies that either a = 0 or b = 0 (the zero-product property.) That is, it is a nontrivial ring without left or right zero divisors. A commutative _____ is called an integral _____.

a. Partially-ordered ring	b. Coherent ring
c. Domain	d. Subring

7. The _____ is often met for the first time as an operation on a single real function of a single real variable. One of the simplest settings for generalizations is to vector valued functions of several variables (most often the domain forms a vector space as well.) This is the field of multivariable calculus.

a. 2-bridge knot	b. -equivalence
c. Derivative	d. -module

8. In linear algebra and functional analysis, a _____ is a linear transformation P from a vector space to itself such that $P^2 = P$. It leaves its image unchanged. Though abstract, this definition of '_____' formalizes and generalizes the idea of graphical _____.

a. Lumer-Phillips theorem	b. C_0-semigroup
c. Convolution power	d. Projection

9. In geometry and linear algebra, a _____ is a transformation in a plane or in space that describes the motion of a rigid body around a fixed point. A _____ is different from a translation, which has no fixed points, and from a reflection, which 'flips' the bodies it is transforming. A _____ and the above-mentioned transformations are isometries; they leave the distance between any two points unchanged after the transformation.

a. Real matrices	b. Shear mappings
c. Reflection	d. Rotation

10. In linear algebra, a _____ is any matrix that acts as a rotation of Euclidean space. For example, the matrix

$$\begin{bmatrix} \cos\theta & -\sin\theta \\ \sin\theta & \cos\theta \end{bmatrix}$$

rotates vectors in the plane counterclockwise by an angle of θ. In three dimensions, rotation matrices are among the simplest algebraic descriptions of rotations, and are used extensively for computations in geometry, physics, and computer graphics.

a. 9-j symbols	b. Rotational symmetry
c. Spin magnetic moment	d. Rotation matrix

11. The notion _____ is used in different, but similar ways:

A permutation P over a set S with k elements is called a _____ with offset t if and only if

the elements of S may be ordered (c < c < ... < c[k]) and the mapping of P may be written as:

p(c[i]) = c[i + t] for i = 1, 2, ..., k − t, and

p(c[i]) = c[i + t − k] for i = k − t + 1, k − t + 2, ..., k.

Chapter 7. Linear Transformations

Note: Every _____ of definition type 1 will be constructed with exactly gcd (k, t) disjoint cycles; see cycles and fixed points.

a. Linear span
c. Near-ring
b. Cycle graph
d. Cyclic permutation

12. In linear algebra, the _____ of a matrix A is another matrix A^T (also written A', A^{tr} or ^tA) created by any one of the following equivalent actions:

- write the rows of A as the columns of A^T
- write the columns of A as the rows of A^T
- reflect A by its main diagonal (which starts from the top left) to obtain A^T

Formally, the _____ of an m × n matrix A with elements A_{ij} is the n × m matrix

$$A^T_{ij} = A_{ji} \text{ for } 1 \leq i \leq n, 1 \leq j \leq m.$$

The _____ of a scalar is the same scalar.

- $\begin{bmatrix} 1 & 2 \end{bmatrix}^T = \begin{bmatrix} 1 \\ 2 \end{bmatrix}.$

- $\begin{bmatrix} 1 & 2 \\ 3 & 4 \end{bmatrix}^T = \begin{bmatrix} 1 & 3 \\ 2 & 4 \end{bmatrix}.$

- $\begin{bmatrix} 1 & 2 \\ 3 & 4 \\ 5 & 6 \end{bmatrix}^T = \begin{bmatrix} 1 & 3 & 5 \\ 2 & 4 & 6 \end{bmatrix}.$

For matrices A, B and scalar c we have the following properties of _____:

1. $\left(\mathbf{A}^T\right)^T = \mathbf{A}$

   Taking the _____ is an involution (self inverse.)

- $(\mathbf{A} + \mathbf{B})^T = \mathbf{A}^T + \mathbf{B}^T$

Chapter 7. Linear Transformations

The _____ respects addition.

- $(\mathbf{AB})^\mathrm{T} = \mathbf{B}^\mathrm{T}\mathbf{A}^\mathrm{T}$

    Note that the order of the factors reverses. From this one can deduce that a square matrix A is invertible if and only if A^T is invertible, and in this case we have $(A^{-1})^\mathrm{T} = (A^\mathrm{T})^{-1}$. It is relatively easy to extend this result to the general case of multiple matrices, where we find that $(ABC...XYZ)^\mathrm{T} = Z^\mathrm{T}Y^\mathrm{T}X^\mathrm{T}...C^\mathrm{T}B^\mathrm{T}A^\mathrm{T}$.

- $(c\mathbf{A})^\mathrm{T} = c\mathbf{A}^\mathrm{T}$

    The _____ of a scalar is the same scalar. Together with (2), this states that the _____ is a linear map from the space of m × n matrices to the space of all n × m matrices.

- $\det(\mathbf{A}^\mathrm{T}) = \det(\mathbf{A})$

    The determinant of a square matrix is the same as that of its _____.

- The dot product of two column vectors a and b can be computed as

$$\mathbf{a} \cdot \mathbf{b} = \mathbf{a}^\mathrm{T}\mathbf{b},$$

which is written as $a_i\, b^i$ in Einstein notation.
- If A has only real entries, then $A^\mathrm{T}A$ is a positive-semidefinite matrix.
- $(\mathbf{A}^\mathrm{T})^{-1} = (\mathbf{A}^{-1})^\mathrm{T}$

    The _____ of an invertible matrix is also invertible, and its inverse is the _____ of the inverse of the original matrix.

- If A is a square matrix, then its eigenvalues are equal to the eigenvalues of its _____.

A square matrix whose _____ is equal to itself is called a symmetric matrix; that is, A is symmetric if

$$\mathbf{A}^\mathrm{T} = \mathbf{A}.$$

A square matrix whose _____ is also its inverse is called an orthogonal matrix; that is, G is orthogonal if

$$\mathbf{G}\mathbf{G}^\mathrm{T} = \mathbf{G}^\mathrm{T}\mathbf{G} = \mathbf{I}_n$$, the identity matrix, i.e. $G^\mathrm{T} = G^{-1}$.

A square matrix whose _____ is equal to its negative is called skew-symmetric matrix; that is, A is skew-symmetric if

$$\mathbf{A}^\mathrm{T} = -\mathbf{A}.$$

The conjugate _____ of the complex matrix A, written as A*, is obtained by taking the _____ of A and the complex conjugate of each entry:

$$\mathbf{A}^* = (\overline{\mathbf{A}})^\mathrm{T} = \overline{(\mathbf{A}^\mathrm{T})}.$$

If f: V→W is a linear map between vector spaces V and W with nondegenerate bilinear forms, we define the _____ of f to be the linear map $^t f$: W→V, determined by

$$B_V(v, {}^t f(w)) = B_W(f(v), w) \quad \forall \, v \in V, w \in W.$$

Here, B_V and B_W are the bilinear forms on V and W respectively. The matrix of the _____ of a map is the transposed matrix only if the bases are orthonormal with respect to their bilinear forms.

Over a complex vector space, one often works with sesquilinear forms instead of bilinear (conjugate-linear in one argument.)

a. Tridiagonal matrix
c. Levinson recursion
b. Drazin inverse
d. Transpose

13. In several fields of mathematics the term _____ is used with different but closely related meanings. They all relate to the notion of mapping the elements of a set to other elements of the same set, i.e., exchanging (or 'permuting') elements of a set.

The general concept of _____ can be defined more formally in different contexts:

In combinatorics, a _____ is usually understood to be a sequence containing each element from a finite set once, and only once.

a. Binary function
c. Permutation
b. Near-field
d. Rupture field

14. In mathematics, the _____, denoted by ⊗, is an operation on two matrices of arbitrary size resulting in a block matrix. It is a special case of a tensor product. The _____ should not be confused with the usual matrix multiplication, which is an entirely different operation.

a. Schur decomposition
c. Kronecker product
b. Totally positive matrix
d. Laplace expansion

Chapter 7. Linear Transformations

15. The column _____ of a matrix A is the maximal number of linearly independent columns of A. Likewise, the row _____ is the maximal number of linearly independent rows of A.

Since the column _____ and the row _____ are always equal, they are simply called the _____ of A. More abstractly, it is the dimension of the image of A. For the proofs, see, e.g., Murase (1960), Andrea ' Wong (1960), Williams ' Cater (1968), Mackiw (1995).) It is commonly denoted by either rk(A) or _____ A.

a. Schur complement
b. Generalized Pauli matrices
c. Rank
d. Split-complex number

16. In mathematics, the _____, denoted by ⊗, may be applied in different contexts to vectors, matrices, tensors, vector spaces, algebras, topological vector spaces, and modules. In each case the significance of the symbol is the same: the most general bilinear operation. In some contexts, this product is also referred to as outer product.

a. Linear span
b. Cycle graph
c. Near-semiring
d. Tensor product

17. In mathematics, the _____ for a Euclidean space consists of one unit vector pointing in the direction of each axis of the Cartesian coordinate system. For example, the _____ for the Euclidean plane are the vectors

$$\mathbf{e}_x = (1,0), \quad \mathbf{e}_y = (0,1),$$

and the _____ for three-dimensional space are the vectors

$$\mathbf{e}_x = (1,0,0), \quad \mathbf{e}_y = (0,1,0), \quad \mathbf{e}_z = (0,0,1).$$

Here the vector e_x points in the x direction, the vector e_y points in the y direction, and the vector e_z points in the z direction. There are several common notations for these vectors, including $\{e_x, e_y, e_z\}$, $\{e_1, e_2, e_3\}$, $\{i, j, k\}$, and $\{x, y, z\}$.

a. -equivalence
b. 2-bridge knot
c. -module
d. Standard basis

18. In mathematics, the _____ is a specific kind of Fourier transform, used in Fourier analysis. It transforms one function into another, which is called the frequency domain representation, or simply the _____, of the original function (which is often a function in the time domain.) But the _____ requires an input function that is discrete and whose non-zero values have a limited (finite) duration.

a. Multitaper
b. Discrete Fourier Transform
c. Modulated complex lapped transform
d. Fourier transform on finite groups

19. In mathematics, the linear algebra concept of _____ can be applied in the context of a finite extension L/K, by using the field trace. This requires the property that the field trace $Tr_{L/K}$ provides a non-degenerate quadratic form over K. This can be guaranteed if the extension is separable; it is automatically true if K is a perfect field, and hence in the cases where K is finite, or of characteristic zero.

A _____ isn't a concrete basis like the polynomial basis or the normal basis; rather it provides a way of using a second basis for computations.

a. Column space
b. Segre classification
c. Linear complementarity problem
d. Dual basis

20. In mathematics, particularly matrix theory and combinatorics, the _____ is an infinite matrix containing the binomial coefficients as its elements. There are 3 ways this can be achieved - either as an upper-triangular matrix, a lower-triangular matrix, or as a symmetric matrix. The 5×5 truncations of these are shown below.

a. Butson-type
b. Conference matrix
c. Polynomial matrix
d. Pascal matrix

21. In mathematics, a _____ is a square matrix whose entries are either +1 or −1 and whose rows are mutually orthogonal. In geometric terms, this means that every two different rows in a _____ represent two perpendicular vectors, while in combinatorial terms, it means that every two different rows have matching entries in exactly half of their columns and mismatched entries in the remaining columns. It is a consequence of this definition that the corresponding properties hold for columns as well as rows.

a. -module
b. 2-bridge knot
c. -equivalence
d. Hadamard matrix

22. In linear algebra, a _____ is a square matrix in which the entries outside the main diagonal (↓) are all zero. The diagonal entries themselves may or may not be zero. Thus, the matrix D = $(d_{i,j})$ with n columns and n rows is diagonal if:

$$d_{i,j} = 0 \text{ if } i \neq j \quad \forall i,j \in \{1, 2, \ldots, n\}.$$

For example, the following matrix is diagonal:

$$\begin{bmatrix} 1 & 0 & 0 \\ 0 & 4 & 0 \\ 0 & 0 & -3 \end{bmatrix}.$$

The term _____ may sometimes refer to a rectangular _____, which is an m-by-n matrix with only the entries of the form $d_{i,i}$ possibly non-zero; for example,

$$\begin{bmatrix} 1 & 0 & 0 \\ 0 & 4 & 0 \\ 0 & 0 & -3 \\ 0 & 0 & 0 \end{bmatrix}, \text{ or}$$

a. Hessenberg matrix	b. Levinson recursion
c. Matrix representation	d. Diagonal matrix

23. For each _____ of a linear transformation, there is a corresponding scalar value called an eigenvalue for that vector, which determines the amount the _____ is scaled under the linear transformation. For example, an eigenvalue of +2 means that the _____ is doubled in length and points in the same direction. An eigenvalue of +1 means that the _____ is unchanged, while an eigenvalue of −1 means that the _____ is reversed in sense.

a. ADE classification	b. Abelian P-root group
c. AKS primality test	d. Eigenvector

24. In linear algebra, two n-by-n matrices A and B are called _____ if

$$B = P^{-1}AP$$

for some invertible n-by-n matrix P. _____ matrices represent the same linear transformation under two different bases, with P being the change of basis matrix.

The matrix P is sometimes called a similarity transformation. In the context of matrix groups, similarity is sometimes referred to as conjugacy, with _____ matrices being conjugate.

a. Cartan matrix	b. Skew-symmetric
c. Zero matrix	d. Similar

25. One of the meanings of the terms _____ and _____ transformation (also called dilation) of a Euclidean space is a function f from the space into itself that multiplies all distances by the same positive scalar r, so that for any two points x and y we have

$$d(f(x), f(y)) = rd(x, y),$$

where 'd(x,y)' is the Euclidean distance from x to y. Two sets are called similar if one is the image of the other under such a _____.

A special case is a homothetic transformation or central _____: it neither involves rotation nor taking the mirror image.

a. -module	b. Similarity
c. Plane	d. -equivalence

26. The matrix P is sometimes called a _____. In the context of matrix groups, similarity is sometimes referred to as conjugacy, with similar matrices being conjugate.

Similarity is an equivalence relation on the space of square matrices.

a. 2-bridge knot
c. -equivalence
b. Similarity transformation
d. -module

27. In mathematics, in particular functional analysis, the _____, or s-numbers of a compact operator T acting on a Hilbert space are defined as the eigenvalues of the operator $\sqrt{T^*T}$ (where T* denotes the adjoint of T and the square root is taken in the operator sense.) The _____ are nonnegative real numbers, usually listed in decreasing order $s_1(T)$, $s_2(T)$, ...

a. Singular values
c. 2-bridge knot
b. -equivalence
d. -module

28. In linear algebra, the _____ is an important factorization of a rectangular real or complex matrix, with several applications in signal processing and statistics. Applications which employ the _____ include computing the pseudoinverse, least squares fitting of data, matrix approximation, and determining the rank, range and null space of a matrix.

Suppose M is an m-by-n matrix whose entries come from the field K, which is either the field of real numbers or the field of complex numbers.

a. 2-bridge knot
c. -equivalence
b. Singular Value Decomposition
d. -module

29. In mathematics, particularly in linear algebra and functional analysis, the _____ of a matrix or linear operator is a factorization analogous to the polar form of a nonzero complex number z

$$z = re^{i\theta}$$

where r is the absolute value of z (a positive real number), and $e^{i\theta}$ is called the complex sign of z.

The _____ of a complex matrix A is a matrix decomposition of the form

$$A = UP$$

where U is a unitary matrix and P is a positive-semidefinite Hermitian matrix. This decomposition always exists; and so long as A is invertible, it is unique, with P positive-definite.

a. Cholesky decomposition
c. Riesz-Thorin theorem
b. Positive definite function on a group
d. Polar decomposition

30. If B(x, x) ≥ 0 for all x, B is said to be positive _____. Negative _____ bilinear forms are defined similarly.

As an example, let V=R², and consider the bilinear form

$$B(x,y) = c_1 x_1 y_1 + c_2 x_2 y_2$$

where $x = (x_1, x_2)$, $y = (y_1, y_2)$, and c_1 and c_2 are constants.

a. -equivalence
b. 2-bridge knot
c. -module
d. Semidefinite

31. In mathematics, a _____ of a number x is a number r such that $r^2 = x$, or, in other words, a number r whose square (the result of multiplying the number by itself) is x.

Every non-negative real number x has a unique non-negative _____, called the principal _____, which is denoted with a radical symbol as $\sqrt{x}$, or, using exponent notation, as $x^{1/2}$. For example, the principal _____ of 9 is 3, denoted $\sqrt{9} = 3$, because $3^2 = 3 \times 3 = 9$.

a. -equivalence
b. -module
c. 2-bridge knot
d. Square root

32. In mathematics, a _____ of a number x is any number which, when repeatedly multiplied by itself, eventually yields x:

$$r \times r \times \cdots \times r = x.$$

In terms of exponentiation, r is a _____ of x if

$$r^n = x$$

for some positive integer n. For example, 2 is a _____ of 16 since $2^4 = 2 \times 2 \times 2 \times 2 = 16$.

The number n is called the degree of the _____.

a. Root
b. Difference of two squares
c. Rationalisation
d. Cubic function

33. In mathematics, a generalized inverse or _____ of a matrix A is a matrix that has some properties of the inverse matrix of A but not necessarily all of them. The term 'the _____' commonly means the Moore-Penrose _____.

The purpose of constructing a generalized inverse is to obtain a matrix that can serve as the inverse in some sense for a wider class of matrices than invertible ones.

a. 2-bridge knot
b. -equivalence
c. Pseudoinverse
d. -module

34. The method of _____ is used to approximately solve overdetermined systems, i.e. systems of equations in which there are more equations than unknowns. _____ is often applied in statistical contexts, particularly regression analysis.

_____ can be interpreted as a method of fitting data.

a. -equivalence
b. -module
c. Least squares
d. 2-bridge knot

Chapter 8. Applications

1. In geometry, a _____ is a straight curve. When geometry is used to model the real world, lines are used to represent straight objects with negligible width and height. Lines are an idealisation of such objects and have no width or height at all and are usually considered to be infinitely long.
   a. -module
   b. 2-bridge knot
   c. -equivalence
   d. Line

2. In geometry, a _____ is a surface of revolution in the shape of a helix with thickness, generated by revolving a circle about the path of a helix. The torus is a special case of the _____ obtained when the helix is crushed to a circle.

   A _____ wrapped around the z-axis can be defined parametrically by:

   $$x(u, v) = (R + r\cos v)\cos u,$$
   $$y(u, v) = (R + r\cos v)\sin u,$$
   $$z(u, v) = r\sin v + \frac{P \cdot u}{\pi},$$

   where

   $u \in [0,\ 2n\pi]\ (n \in \mathbb{R})$,
   $v \in [0,\ 2\pi]$,
   R is the distance from the center of the tube to the center of the helix,
   r is the radius of the tube,
   P is the speed of the movement along the z axis (in a right-handed Cartesian coordinate system, positive values create right-handed springs, whereas negative values create left-handed springs),
   n is the number of rounds in circle.

   a. Spring
   b. PDE surfaces
   c. Steiner surfaces
   d. Ruled surfaces

3. The most commonly encountered form of Hooke's law is probably the spring equation, which relates the force exerted by a spring to the distance it is stretched by a _____, k, measured in force per length.

   $$F = -kx$$

   The negative sign indicates that the force exerted by the spring is in direct opposition to the direction of displacement. It is called a 'restoring force', as it tends to restore the system to equilibrium.

   a. 2-bridge knot
   b. Spring constant
   c. -equivalence
   d. -module

4. _____ is a branch of mathematics that concerns itself with the mathematical techniques typically used in the application of mathematical knowledge to other domains.

There is no consensus of what the various branches of _____ are. Such categorizations are made difficult by the way mathematics and science change over time, and also by the way universities organize departments, courses, and degrees.

a. ADE classification
c. Applied mathematics
b. Abelian P-root group
d. AKS primality test

5. In theory of probability, a _____ is an equation that describes the flux in and the flux out of states of a Markov chain.

The global balance equations are a set are a set of equations that in principal can always be solved to give the equilibrium/steady state distribution of a Markov chain (when such a distribution exists.) For a Markov chain with state space S, transition rate from state n to m given by q(n,m) and equilibrium distribution given by π, the global balance equations are given for every state n in S by

$$\sum_{n \in S} \pi(n)q(n,m) = \sum_{n \in S} \pi(m)q(m,n).$$

Some Markov processes satisfy a particularly convenient property known as local balance (also independent balance or partial balance.)

a. 2-bridge knot
c. Balance equation
b. -equivalence
d. -module

6. The _____ is a numerical technique for finding approximate solutions of partial differential equations (PDE) as well as of integral equations. The solution approach is based either on eliminating the differential equation completely (steady state problems), or rendering the PDE into an approximating system of ordinary differential equations, which are then numerically integrated using standard techniques such as Euler's method, Runge-Kutta, etc.

In solving partial differential equations, the primary challenge is to create an equation that approximates the equation to be studied, but is numerically stable, meaning that errors in the input data and intermediate calculations do not accumulate and cause the resulting output to be meaningless.

a. Finite element method
c. -module
b. -equivalence
d. 2-bridge knot

7. A _____ is a matrix in which all the elements are greater than zero. The set of positive matrices is a subset of all non-negative matrices.

A non-negative matrix can represent a transition matrix for a Markov chain.

a. 2-bridge knot
c. -equivalence
b. Positive matrix
d. -module

Chapter 8. Applications

8. In mathematics, a _____ is a rectangular array of numbers. This way, matrices can record data that depend on multiple parameters. In particular they are used to keep track of the coefficients of multiple linear equations. Matrices are closely connected to linear transformations, which are higher-dimensional analogs of linear functions, i.e., functions of the form f(x) = c Â· x, where c is a constant. This map corresponds to a _____ with one row and column, with entry c. In addition to a number of elementary, entrywise operations such as _____ addition a key notion is _____ multiplication, which displays a number of features not encountered in numbers; for example, products of matrices depend on the order of the factors, unlike products of real numbers, say, where c Â· d = d Â· c for any two numbers c and d.

a. Polynomial expression
b. Commutativity
c. Heap
d. Matrix

9. In linear algebra, a basis for a vector space of dimension n is a sequence of n vectors $α_1, ..., α_n$ with the property that every vector in the space can be expressed uniquely as a linear combination of the basis vectors. Since it is often desirable to work with more than one basis for a vector space, it is of fundamental importance in linear algebra to be able to easily transform coordinate-wise representations of vectors and linear transformations taken with respect to one basis to their equivalent representations with respect to another basis. Such a transformation is called a _____.

a. Change of basis
b. Split-complex number
c. Generalized singular value decomposition
d. Field of values

10. In linear algebra, a _____ is a set of vectors that, in a linear combination, can represent every vector in a given vector space or free module, and such that no element of the set can be represented as a linear combination of the others. In other words, a _____ is a linearly independent spanning set.

a. Minor
b. Chirality
c. Supergroup
d. Basis

11. If B(x, x) ≥ 0 for all x, B is said to be positive _____. Negative _____ bilinear forms are defined similarly.

As an example, let $V=R^2$, and consider the bilinear form

$$B(x,y) = c_1 x_1 y_1 + c_2 x_2 y_2$$

where $x = (x_1, x_2)$, $y = (y_1, y_2)$, and c_1 and c_2 are constants.

a. 2-bridge knot
b. Semidefinite
c. -equivalence
d. -module

12. In mathematics, in the field of differential equations, a boundary value problem is a differential equation together with a set of additional restraints, called the _____. A solution to a boundary value problem is a solution to the differential equation which also satisfies the _____.

Boundary value problems arise in several branches of physics as any physical differential equation will have them.

a. Boundary conditions
b. -equivalence
c. -module
d. 2-bridge knot

13. In mathematics, a _____ maps a function, $f(x)$, to another function, $f(x + b) - f(x + a)$.

The forward _____

$$\Delta f(x) = f(x+1) - f(x)$$

occurs frequently in the calculus of finite differences, where it plays a role formally similar to that of the derivative, but used in discrete circumstances. Difference equations can often be solved with techniques very similar to those for solving differential equations.

a. 2-bridge knot
c. -equivalence
b. Difference operator
d. -module

14. In linear algebra, a _____ matrix is a matrix that is 'almost' a diagonal matrix. To be exact: a _____ matrix has nonzero elements only in the main diagonal, the first diagonal below this, and the first diagonal above the main diagonal.

For example, the following matrix is _____:

$$\begin{pmatrix} 1 & 4 & 0 & 0 \\ 3 & 4 & 1 & 0 \\ 0 & 2 & 3 & 4 \\ 0 & 0 & 1 & 3 \end{pmatrix}.$$

A determinant formed from a _____ matrix is known as a continuant.

a. -equivalence
c. 2-bridge knot
b. -module
d. Tridiagonal

15. In mathematics, an _____ is a matrix that shows the relationship between two classes of objects. If the first class is X and the second is Y, the matrix has one row for each element of X and one column for each element of Y. The entry in row x and column y is 1 if x and y are related (called incident in this context) and 0 if they are not.

a. Incidence matrix
c. Abelian P-root group
b. ADE classification
d. AKS primality test

16. In linear algebra and numerical analysis, a _____ P of a matrix A is a matrix such that $P^{-1}A$ has a smaller condition number than A. Preconditioners are useful when using an iterative method to solve a large, sparse linear system

$$Ax = b$$

for x since the rate of convergence for most iterative linear solvers degrades as the condition number of a matrix increases. Instead of solving the original linear system above, one may solve either the left preconditioned system

$$P^{-1}Ax = P^{-1}b,$$

via the two solves

$$c = P^{-1}b, \qquad (P^{-1}A)x = c,$$

or the right preconditioned system

$$AP^{-1}Px = b,$$

via the two solves

$$(AP^{-1})y = b, \qquad x = P^{-1}y,$$

which are both equivalent to solving the original system so long as the _____ matrix P is nonsingular.

The goal of this preconditioned system is to reduce the condition number of the left or right preconditioned system matrix

$$P^{-1}A,$$

or

$$AP^{-1},$$

respectively.

a. Preconditioner
c. -module
b. -equivalence
d. 2-bridge knot

17. Economics is the social science that studies the production, distribution, and consumption of goods and services. The term economics comes from the Ancient Greek οἰκονομία from οἶκος (oikos, 'house') + νόμος (nomos, 'custom' or 'law'), hence 'rules of the house(hold)'. Current _____ models developed out of the broader field of political economy in the late 19th century, owing to a desire to use an empirical approach more akin to the physical sciences.

a. ADE classification
c. Abelian P-root group
b. AKS primality test
d. Economic

18. In mathematics, a _____ is a series with a constant ratio between successive terms. For example, the series

$$\frac{1}{2} + \frac{1}{4} + \frac{1}{8} + \frac{1}{16} + \cdots$$

is geometric, because each term is equal to half of the previous term. The sum of this series is 1, as illustrated in the following picture:

_____ are one of the simplest examples of infinite series with finite sums.

a. -equivalence
b. 2-bridge knot
c. Geometric series
d. -module

19. In mathematics, _____ is a technique for optimization of a linear objective function, subject to linear equality and linear inequality constraints. Informally, _____ determines the way to achieve the best outcome (such as maximum profit or lowest cost) in a given mathematical model and given some list of requirements represented as linear equations.

More formally, given a polytope (for example, a polygon or a polyhedron), and a real-valued affine function

$$f(x_1, x_2, \ldots, x_n) = c_1 x_1 + c_2 x_2 + \cdots + c_n x_n + d$$

defined on this polytope, a _____ method will find a point in the polytope where this function has the smallest (or largest) value.

a. -equivalence
b. -module
c. 2-bridge knot
d. Linear programming

20. An unrelated, but similarly named method is the Nelder-Mead method or downhill _____ due to Nelder ' Mead (1965) and is a numerical method for optimizing many-dimensional unconstrained problems, belonging to the more general class of search algorithms.

In both cases, the method uses the concept of a simplex, which is a polytope of N + 1 vertices in N dimensions: a line segment in one dimension, a triangle in two dimensions, a tetrahedron in three-dimensional space and so forth.

A system of linear inequalities defines a polytope as a feasible region.

a. -equivalence
b. 2-bridge knot
c. -module
d. Simplex method

21. In linear programming, the primary problem and the _____ are complementary. A solution to either one determines a solution to both.

Linear programming problems are optimization problems in which the objective function and the constraints are all linear.

a. -module
b. 2-bridge knot
c. -equivalence
d. Dual problem

22. The _____ of an angle is the ratio of the length of the adjacent side to the length of the hypotenuse. In our case

$$\cos A = \frac{\text{adjacent}}{\text{hypotenuse}} = \frac{b}{h}.$$

The tangent of an angle is the ratio of the length of the opposite side to the length of the adjacent side. In our case

$$\tan A = \frac{\text{opposite}}{\text{adjacent}} = \frac{a}{b}.$$

The remaining three functions are best defined using the above three functions.

a. 2-bridge knot
b. -module
c. -equivalence
d. Cosine

23. In mathematics, the Cauchy-_____ the Cauchy inequality is a useful inequality encountered in many different settings, such as linear algebra applied to vectors, in analysis applied to infinite series and integration of products, and in probability theory, applied to variances and covariances. The general formulation of the Heisenberg uncertainty principle is derived using the Cauchy-_____ in the Hilbert space of pure quantum states.

The inequality for sums was published by , while the corresponding inequality for integrals was first stated by and rediscovered by

a. Schwarz inequality
b. 2-bridge knot
c. -equivalence
d. -module

24. In mathematics, an _____ is a statement about the relative size or order of two objects, or about whether they are the same or not

- The notation a < b means that a is less than b.
- The notation a > b means that a is greater than b.
- The notation a ≠ b means that a is not equal to b, but does not say that one is bigger than the other or even that they can be compared in size.

In all these cases, a is not equal to b, hence, '_____'.

These relations are known as strict _____

- The notation a ≤ b means that a is less than or equal to b (or, equivalently, not greater than b);
- The notation a ≥ b means that a is greater than or equal to b (or, equivalently, not smaller than b);

Chapter 8. Applications

An additional use of the notation is to show that one quantity is much greater than another, normally by several orders of magnitude.

- The notation a ≪ b means that a is much less than b.
- The notation a ≫ b means that a is much greater than b.

If the sense of the _____ is the same for all values of the variables for which its members are defined, then the _____ is called an 'absolute' or 'unconditional' _____. If the sense of an _____ holds only for certain values of the variables involved, but is reversed or destroyed for other values of the variables, it is called a conditional _____.

One can apply the same algebraic operations to inequalities as one would apply for solving equalities. For example, to find x for the _____ 10x > 20 one would divide 20 by 10 to obtain x > 2.

a. Inequality
c. ADE classification
b. Abelian P-root group
d. AKS primality test

25. In mathematics, a _____ decomposes a periodic function or periodic signal into a sum of simple oscillating functions, namely sines and cosines. The study of _____ is a branch of Fourier analysis. _____ were introduced by Joseph Fourier (1768-1830) for the purpose of solving the heat equation in a metal plate.

a. -module
c. -equivalence
b. 2-bridge knot
d. Fourier series

26. In mathematics, a _____ is a set of functions of a given kind from a set X to a set Y. It is called a space because in many applications, it is a topological space or a vector space or both.

Function spaces appear in various areas of mathematics:

- in set theory, the power set of a set X may be identified with the set of all functions from X to {0,1};, denoted 2^X. More generally, the set of functions $X \rightarrow Y$ is denoted Y^X.

- in linear algebra the set of all linear transformations from a vector space V to another one, W, over the same field, is itself a vector space;

- in functional analysis the same is seen for continuous linear transformations, including topologies on the vector spaces in the above, and many of the major examples are function spaces carrying a topology; the best known examples include Hilbert spaces and Banach spaces.

- in functional analysis the set of all functions from the natural numbers to some set X is called a sequence space. It consists of the set of all possible sequences of elements of X.

- in topology, one may attempt to put a topology on the space of continuous functions from a topological space X to another one Y, with utility depending on the nature of the spaces. A commonly used example is the compact-open topology, e.g. loop space.

a. -module
b. Function space
c. -equivalence
d. 2-bridge knot

27. In abstract algebra, the _____ of a module is a measure of the module's 'size'. It is defined as the _____ of the longest ascending chain of submodules and is a generalization of the concept of dimension for vector spaces. The modules with finite _____ share many important properties with finite-dimensional vector spaces.
    a. Finitely generated module
    b. Length
    c. Morita equivalence
    d. Supermodule

28. In mathematics, two vectors are _____ if they are perpendicular, i.e., they form a right angle. The word comes from the Greek ὀρθός , meaning 'straight', and γωνία (gonia), meaning 'angle'. For example, a subway and the street above, although they do not physically intersect, are _____ if they cross at a right angle.
    a. Expression
    b. Embedding
    c. Orthogonal
    d. Unital

29. The _____ is often met for the first time as an operation on a single real function of a single real variable. One of the simplest settings for generalizations is to vector valued functions of several variables (most often the domain forms a vector space as well.) This is the field of multivariable calculus.
    a. -module
    b. 2-bridge knot
    c. -equivalence
    d. Derivative

30. In linear algebra and functional analysis, a _____ is a linear transformation P from a vector space to itself such that $P^2 = P$. It leaves its image unchanged. Though abstract, this definition of '_____' formalizes and generalizes the idea of graphical _____.
    a. Convolution power
    b. Lumer-Phillips theorem
    c. Projection
    d. C_0-semigroup

1. In numerical analysis, the _____ associated with a problem is a measure of that problem's amenability to digital computation, that is, how numerically well-conditioned the problem is. A problem with a low _____ is said to be well-conditioned, while a problem with a high _____ is said to be ill-conditioned.

For example, the _____ associated with the linear equation Ax = b gives a bound on how inaccurate the solution x will be after approximate solution.

a. -equivalence
b. -module
c. Condition number
d. Bernstein polynomial

2. In the case of Gaussian elimination, it is best to choose a pivot element with large absolute value. This improves the numerical stability. In _____, the algorithm considers all entries in the column of the matrix that is currently being considered, picks the entry with largest absolute value, and finally swaps rows such that this entry is the pivot in question.

a. -module
b. -equivalence
c. 2-bridge knot
d. Partial pivoting

3. In its simplest meaning in mathematics and logic, an _____ is an action or procedure which produces a new value from one or more input values. There are two common types of operations: unary and binary. Unary operations involve only one value, such as negation and trigonometric functions.

a. ADE classification
b. Operation
c. Abelian P-root group
d. AKS primality test

4. In mathematics, a _____ is a semigroup in which every element is idempotent The lattice of varieties of bands was described independently by Birjukov, Fennemore and Gerhard. Semilattices, left-zero bands, right-zero bands, rectangular bands and regular bands, specific subclasses of bands which lie near the bottom of this lattice, are of particular interest and are briefly described below.

a. Direct product
b. Formal power series
c. Group extension
d. Band

5. In mathematics, particularly matrix theory, a _____ is a sparse matrix, whose non-zero entries are confined to a diagonal band, comprising the main diagonal and zero or more diagonals on either side.

Formally, an n×n matrix A=($a_{i,j}$) is a _____ if all matrix elements are zero outside a diagonally bordered band whose range is determined by constants k_1 and k_2:

$$a_{i,j} = 0 \quad \text{if} \quad j < i - k_1 \quad \text{or} \quad j > i + k_2; \quad k_1, k_2 \geq 0.$$

The quantities k_1 and k_2 are the left and right half-bandwidth, respectively. The bandwidth of the matrix is $k_1 + k_2 + 1$ (in other words, the smallest number of adjacent diagonals to which the non-zero elements are confined.)

a. Skew-symmetric
b. Band matrix
c. Modal matrix
d. Binary matrix

6. In mathematics, a _____ is a rectangular array of numbers. This way, matrices can record data that depend on multiple parameters. In particular they are used to keep track of the coefficients of multiple linear equations. Matrices are closely connected to linear transformations, which are higher-dimensional analogs of linear functions, i.e., functions of the form f(x) = c Â· x, where c is a constant. This map corresponds to a _____ with one row and column, with entry c. In addition to a number of elementary, entrywise operations such as _____ addition a key notion is _____ multiplication, which displays a number of features not encountered in numbers; for example, products of matrices depend on the order of the factors, unlike products of real numbers, say, where c Â· d = d Â· c for any two numbers c and d.

a. Commutativity
b. Heap
c. Matrix
d. Polynomial expression

7. In geometry and linear algebra, a _____ is a transformation in a plane or in space that describes the motion of a rigid body around a fixed point. A _____ is different from a translation, which has no fixed points, and from a reflection, which 'flips' the bodies it is transforming. A _____ and the above-mentioned transformations are isometries; they leave the distance between any two points unchanged after the transformation.

a. Shear mappings
b. Real matrices
c. Rotation
d. Reflection

8. In linear algebra, a _____ is any matrix that acts as a rotation of Euclidean space. For example, the matrix

$$\begin{bmatrix} \cos\theta & -\sin\theta \\ \sin\theta & \cos\theta \end{bmatrix}$$

rotates vectors in the plane counterclockwise by an angle of θ. In three dimensions, rotation matrices are among the simplest algebraic descriptions of rotations, and are used extensively for computations in geometry, physics, and computer graphics.

a. 9-j symbols
b. Rotational symmetry
c. Spin magnetic moment
d. Rotation matrix

9. In linear algebra, a _____ is a square matrix with entries being the unit fractions

$$H_{ij} = \frac{1}{i+j-1}.$$

For example, this is the 5 × 5 _____:

$$H = \begin{bmatrix} 1 & \frac{1}{2} & \frac{1}{3} & \frac{1}{4} & \frac{1}{5} \\ \frac{1}{2} & \frac{1}{3} & \frac{1}{4} & \frac{1}{5} & \frac{1}{6} \\ \frac{1}{3} & \frac{1}{4} & \frac{1}{5} & \frac{1}{6} & \frac{1}{7} \\ \frac{1}{4} & \frac{1}{5} & \frac{1}{6} & \frac{1}{7} & \frac{1}{8} \\ \frac{1}{5} & \frac{1}{6} & \frac{1}{7} & \frac{1}{8} & \frac{1}{9} \end{bmatrix}.$$

The _____ can be regarded as derived from the integral

$$H_{ij} = \int_0^1 x^{i+j-2}\, dx,$$

that is, as a Gramian matrix for powers of x. It arises in the least squares approximation of arbitrary functions by polynomials.

The Hilbert matrices are canonical examples of ill-conditioned matrices, making them notoriously difficult to use in numerical computation.

a. Triangular matrix
b. Minimum degree algorithm
c. Diagonally dominant
d. Hilbert matrix

10. The _____ were developed by Leonhard Euler to describe the orientation of a rigid body (a body in which the relative position of all its points is constant) in 3-dimensional Euclidean space. To give an object a specific orientation it may be subjected to a sequence of three rotations described by the _____. This is equivalent to saying that a rotation matrix can be decomposed as a product of three elemental rotations.

a. ADE classification
b. Euler angles
c. AKS primality test
d. Abelian P-root group

11. In linear algebra, functional analysis and related areas of mathematics, a _____ is a function that assigns a strictly positive length or size to all vectors in a vector space, other than the zero vector. A seminorm (or pseudonorm), on the other hand, is allowed to assign zero length to some non-zero vectors.

A simple example is the 2-dimensional Euclidean space R^2 equipped with the Euclidean _____.

a. -module
b. Quasinorm
c. -equivalence
d. Norm

12. A _____ is one of the basic shapes of geometry: a polygon with three corners or vertices and three sides or edges which are line segments. A _____ with vertices A, B, and C is denoted ABC.

Chapter 9. Numerical Linear Algebra

In Euclidean geometry any three non-collinear points determine a unique _____ and a unique plane (i.e. a two-dimensional Euclidean space.)

a. -module
b. -equivalence
c. Triangle
d. 2-bridge knot

13. In mathematics, the _____ states that for any triangle, the length of a given side must be less than the sum of the other two sides but greater than the difference between the two sides.

In Euclidean geometry and some other geometries this is a theorem. In the Euclidean case, in both the less than or equal to and greater than or equal to statements, equality occurs only if the triangle has a 180° angle and two 0° angles, as shown in the bottom example in the image to the right.

a. 2-bridge knot
b. -module
c. Triangle inequality
d. -equivalence

14. In geometry and trigonometry, an _____ is the figure formed by two rays sharing a common endpoint, called the vertex of the _____ . The magnitude of the _____ is the 'amount of rotation' that separates the two rays, and can be measured by considering the length of circular arc swept out when one ray is rotated about the vertex to coincide with the other Where there is no possibility of confusion, the term '_____' is used interchangeably for both the geometric configuration itself and for its angular magnitude (which is simply a numerical quantity.)

a. ADE classification
b. AKS primality test
c. Abelian P-root group
d. Angle

15. In mathematics, an _____ is a statement about the relative size or order of two objects, or about whether they are the same or not

- The notation a < b means that a is less than b.
- The notation a > b means that a is greater than b.
- The notation a ≠ b means that a is not equal to b, but does not say that one is bigger than the other or even that they can be compared in size.

In all these cases, a is not equal to b, hence, '_____'.

These relations are known as strict _____

- The notation a ≤ b means that a is less than or equal to b (or, equivalently, not greater than b);
- The notation a ≥ b means that a is greater than or equal to b (or, equivalently, not smaller than b);

Chapter 9. Numerical Linear Algebra

An additional use of the notation is to show that one quantity is much greater than another, normally by several orders of magnitude.

- The notation a ≪ b means that a is much less than b.
- The notation a ≫ b means that a is much greater than b.

If the sense of the _____ is the same for all values of the variables for which its members are defined, then the _____ is called an 'absolute' or 'unconditional' _____. If the sense of an _____ holds only for certain values of the variables involved, but is reversed or destroyed for other values of the variables, it is called a conditional _____.

One can apply the same algebraic operations to inequalities as one would apply for solving equalities. For example, to find x for the _____ 10x > 20 one would divide 20 by 10 to obtain x > 2.

a. ADE classification
c. AKS primality test
b. Abelian P-root group
d. Inequality

16. In mathematics, for a given complex Hermitian matrix A and nonzero vector x, the _____ R(A,x) is defined as:

$$\frac{x^* A x}{x^* x}.$$

For real matrices and vectors, the condition of being Hermitian reduces to that of being symmetric, and the conjugate transpose x^* to the usual transpose x'. Note that R(A,cx) = R(A,x) for any real scalar c. Recall that a Hermitian (or real symmetric) matrix has real eigenvalues.

a. Vectorization
c. Projection-valued measure
b. Reality structure
d. Rayleigh quotient

17. In mathematics, in particular functional analysis, the _____, or s-numbers of a compact operator T acting on a Hilbert space are defined as the eigenvalues of the operator $\sqrt{T^*T}$ (where T^* denotes the adjoint of T and the square root is taken in the operator sense.) The _____ are nonnegative real numbers, usually listed in decreasing order $s_1(T)$, $s_2(T)$, ...

a. -module
c. 2-bridge knot
b. -equivalence
d. Singular values

18. In linear algebra, two vectors in an inner product space are _____ if they are orthogonal and both of unit length. A set of vectors form an _____ set if all vectors in the set are mutually orthogonal and all of unit length. An _____ set which forms a basis is called an _____ basis.

a. Elementary matrix
c. Invertible matrix
b. Overdetermined
d. Orthonormal

Chapter 9. Numerical Linear Algebra

19. In mathematics, an _____ of an inner product space V (i.e., a vector space with an inner product), is a set of mutually orthogonal vectors of magnitude 1 (unit vectors) that span the space when infinite linear combinations are allowed. (In some contexts, especially in linear algebra, the concept of basis (linear algebra) means a set of vectors that span a space when only finite linear combinations are allowed.) Such an infinite linear combination is an infinite series, and the concept of convergence relied upon is defined in terms of the space's inner product.
   a. Eigendecomposition
   b. Orthonormal basis
   c. Overdetermined
   d. Orientation

20. One commonly distinguishes between the _____ and the absolute error. The absolute error is the magnitude of the difference between the exact value and the approximation. The _____ is the absolute error divided by the magnitude of the exact value.
   a. 2-bridge knot
   b. Relative error
   c. -equivalence
   d. -module

21. In linear algebra, a _____ is a set of vectors that, in a linear combination, can represent every vector in a given vector space or free module, and such that no element of the set can be represented as a linear combination of the others. In other words, a _____ is a linearly independent spanning set.
   a. Basis
   b. Chirality
   c. Minor
   d. Supergroup

22. In mathematics, the _____ of a matrix or a bounded linear operator is the supremum among the absolute values of the elements in its spectrum, which is sometimes denoted by ρ(Â·.)

Let $\lambda_1, ..., \lambda_s$ be the (real or complex) eigenvalues of a matrix $A \in C^{n \times n}$. Then its _____ ρ(A) is defined as:

$$\rho(A) := \max_i (|\lambda_i|)$$

The following lemma shows a simple yet useful upper bound for the _____ of a matrix:

Lemma: Let $A \in C^{n \times n}$ be a complex-valued matrix, ρ(A) its _____ and ||Â·|| a consistent matrix norm; then, for each k ∈ ℕ:

$$\rho(A) \leq \|A^k\|^{1/k}, \quad \forall k \in \mathbb{N}.$$

Proof: Let (v, λ) be an eigenvector-eigenvalue pair for a matrix A. By the sub-multiplicative property of the matrix norm, we get:

$$|\lambda|^k \|\mathbf{v}\| = \|\lambda^k \mathbf{v}\| = \|A^k \mathbf{v}\| \leq \|A^k\| \cdot \|\mathbf{v}\|$$

and since v ≠ 0 for each λ we have

$$|\lambda|^k \leq \|A^k\|$$

and therefore

$$\rho(A) \leq \|A^k\|^{1/k} \quad \square$$

The _____ is closely related to the behaviour of the convergence of the power sequence of a matrix; namely, the following theorem holds:

Theorem: Let $A \in C^{n \times n}$ be a complex-valued matrix and ρ(A) its _____; then

$$\lim_{k \to \infty} A^k = 0$$

if and only if ρ(A) < 1.

Moreover, if ρ(A)>1, $\|A^k\|$ is not bounded for increasing k values.

a. Spectral geometry
b. Spectral theorem
c. Spectral radius
d. Spectral asymmetry

23. In linear algebra and numerical analysis, a _____ P of a matrix A is a matrix such that $P^{-1}A$ has a smaller condition number than A. Preconditioners are useful when using an iterative method to solve a large, sparse linear system

$$Ax = b$$

for x since the rate of convergence for most iterative linear solvers degrades as the condition number of a matrix increases. Instead of solving the original linear system above, one may solve either the left preconditioned system

$$P^{-1}Ax = P^{-1}b,$$

via the two solves

$$c = P^{-1}b, \qquad (P^{-1}A)x = c,$$

or the right preconditioned system

$$AP^{-1}Px = b,$$

via the two solves

$$(AP^{-1})y = b, \qquad x = P^{-1}y,$$

which are both equivalent to solving the original system so long as the _____ matrix P is nonsingular.

The goal of this preconditioned system is to reduce the condition number of the left or right preconditioned system matrix

$$P^{-1}A,$$

or

$$AP^{-1},$$

respectively.

a. -module
c. 2-bridge knot
b. -equivalence
d. Preconditioner

24. In algebra, a _____ of an element in a quadratic extension field of a field K is its image under the unique non-identity automorphism of the extended field that fixes K. If the extension is generated by a square root of an element r of K, then the _____ of $a + b\sqrt{r}$ is $a - b\sqrt{r}$ for $a, b \in K$, and in particular in the case of the field C of complex numbers as an extension of the field R of real numbers (where r = − 1), the complex _____ of a + bi is a − bi.

Forming the sum or product of any element of the extension field with its _____ always gives an element of K. This can be used to rewrite a quotient of numbers in the extended field so that the denominator lies in K, by multiplying numerator and denominator by the _____ of the denominator. This process is called rationalization of the denominator, in particular if K is the field Q of rational numbers.

a. K-theory
c. Field arithmetic
b. Digital root
d. Conjugate

25. In mathematics, the _____ is an eigenvalue algorithm: given a matrix A, the algorithm will produce a number λ (the eigenvalue) and a nonzero vector v (the eigenvector), such that Av = λv.

The _____ is a very simple algorithm. It does not compute a matrix decomposition, and hence it can be used when A is a very large sparse matrix.

104 Chapter 9. Numerical Linear Algebra

a. -module
c. -equivalence
b. 2-bridge knot
d. Power iteration

26. In numerical linear algebra, the _____ is an eigenvalue algorithm; that is, a procedure to calculate the eigenvalues and eigenvectors of a matrix. The QR transformation was developed in 1961 by John G.F. Francis (England) and by Vera N. Kublanovskaya (USSR), working independently. The basic idea is to perform a QR decomposition, writing the matrix as a product of an orthogonal matrix and an upper triangular matrix, multiply the factors in the other order, and iterate.

a. QR algorithm
c. -equivalence
b. -module
d. 2-bridge knot

27. In linear algebra, a _____ is one that is 'almost' triangular. To be exact, an upper _____ has zero entries below the first subdiagonal, and a lower _____ has zero entries above the first superdiagonal. They are named for Karl Hessenberg.

a. Main diagonal
c. Duplication matrix
b. Hessenberg matrix
d. Paley construction

28. In linear algebra, a _____ matrix is a matrix that is 'almost' a diagonal matrix. To be exact: a _____ matrix has nonzero elements only in the main diagonal, the first diagonal below this, and the first diagonal above the main diagonal.

For example, the following matrix is _____:

$$\begin{pmatrix} 1 & 4 & 0 & 0 \\ 3 & 4 & 1 & 0 \\ 0 & 2 & 3 & 4 \\ 0 & 0 & 1 & 3 \end{pmatrix}.$$

A determinant formed from a _____ matrix is known as a continuant.

a. -module
c. -equivalence
b. 2-bridge knot
d. Tridiagonal

29. In mathematics, a matrix is said to be _____ if in every row of the matrix, the magnitude of the diagonal entry in that row is larger than or equal to the sum of the magnitudes of all the other (non-diagonal) entries in that row, and if in at least one row of the matrix, the magnitude of the diagonal entry in that row is strictly larger than the sum of the magnitudes of all the other (non-diagonal) entries in that row. More precisely, the matrix A is _____ if

<_____>
$$|a_{ii}| \geq \sum_{j \neq i} |a_{ij}| \quad \text{for all } i, \quad |a_{ii}| > \sum_{j \neq i} |a_{ij}| \quad \text{for at least one } i,$$

where a_{ij} denotes the entry in the ith row and jth column. If the strictly greater than equality is true for all rows (all values of i), then the matrix is called strictly _____.

a. Diagonally dominant
c. Minimum degree algorithm
b. Circulant matrix
d. Triangular matrix

30. In mathematics, the _____ may be used to bound the spectrum of a square matrix. It was first published by the Belarusian mathematician Semyon Aranovich Gershgorin in 1931. The spelling of S. A. Gershgorin's name has been transliterated in several different ways, including GerÅÂ¡gorin, Gerschgorin, Gershgorin and Hershhorn/Hirschhorn, the latter corresponding to the transliteration of the Yiddish spelling of his name, which is >×â€ ×â"¢×Â¨×Â©×â€ ×Â ÖÂ¸×Â¨×Â.
a. Lattice theorem
c. Structure theorem for finitely generated modules over a principal ideal domain
b. Malgrange preparation theorem
d. Gershgorin circle theorem

31. In linear algebra, the order-r _____ generated by an n-by-n matrix A and a vector b of dimension n is the linear subspace spanned by the images of b under the first r powers of A (starting from A^0 = I), that is,

$$\mathcal{K}_r(A,b) = \text{span}\{b, Ab, A^2b, \ldots, A^{r-1}b\}.$$

It is named after Russian applied mathematician and naval engineer Alexei Krylov.

Modern iterative methods for finding one eigenvalues of large sparse matrices or solving large systems of linear equations avoid matrix-matrix operations, but rather multiply vectors by the matrix and work with the resulting vectors. Starting with a vector, b, one computes Ab, then one multiplies that vector by A to find A^2b and so on.

a. -equivalence
c. -module
b. 2-bridge knot
d. Krylov subspace

Chapter 10. Complex Vectors and Matrices

1. In mathematics, the complex numbers are an extension of the real numbers obtained by adjoining an imaginary unit, denoted i, which satisfies:

$$i^2 = -1.$$

Every _____ can be written in the form a + bi, where a and b are real numbers called the real part and the imaginary part of the _____, respectively.

Complex numbers are a field, and thus have addition, subtraction, multiplication, and division operations. These operations extend the corresponding operations on real numbers, although with a number of additional elegant and useful properties, e.g., negative real numbers can be obtained by squaring complex (imaginary) numbers.

   a. -equivalence
   b. Complex number
   c. 2-bridge knot
   d. -module

2. In mathematics, the (formal) _____ of a complex vector space V is the complex vector space $\overline{V}$ consisting of all formal complex conjugates of elements of V. That is, $\overline{V}$ is a vector space whose elements are in one-to-one correspondence with the elements of V:

$$\overline{V} = \{\overline{v} \mid v \in V\},$$

with the following rules for addition and scalar multiplication:

$$\overline{v} + \overline{w} = \overline{v + w} \quad \text{and} \quad \alpha \overline{v} = \overline{\overline{\alpha} v}.$$

Here v and w are vectors in V, α is a complex number, and $\overline{\alpha}$ denotes the _____ of α.

In the case where V is a linear subspace of $\mathbb{C}^n$, the formal _____ $\overline{V}$ is naturally isomorphic to the actual _____ subspace of V in $\mathbb{C}^n$.

   a. Complex conjugate
   b. Conjugate transpose
   c. Binomial inverse theorem
   d. Polynomial basis

3. In algebra, a _____ of an element in a quadratic extension field of a field K is its image under the unique non-identity automorphism of the extended field that fixes K. If the extension is generated by a square root of an element r of K, then the _____ of $a + b\sqrt{r}$ is $a - b\sqrt{r}$ for $a, b \in K$, and in particular in the case of the field C of complex numbers as an extension of the field R of real numbers (where r = −1), the complex _____ of a + bi is a − bi.

Forming the sum or product of any element of the extension field with its _____ always gives an element of K. This can be used to rewrite a quotient of numbers in the extended field so that the denominator lies in K, by multiplying numerator and denominator by the _____ of the denominator. This process is called rationalization of the denominator, in particular if K is the field Q of rational numbers.

a. K-theory
c. Field arithmetic
b. Digital root
d. Conjugate

4. _____ is a branch of mathematics that deals with triangles, particularly those plane triangles in which one angle has 90 degrees (right triangles.) _____ deals with relationships between the sides and the angles of triangles and with the trigonometric functions, which describe those relationships.

_____ has applications in both pure mathematics and in applied mathematics, where it is essential in many branches of science and technology.

a. 2-bridge knot
c. Trigonometry
b. -module
d. -equivalence

5. In mathematics, a _____ of a number x is any number which, when repeatedly multiplied by itself, eventually yields x:

$$r \times r \times \cdots \times r = x.$$

In terms of exponentiation, r is a _____ of x if

$$r^n = x$$

for some positive integer n. For example, 2 is a _____ of 16 since $2^4 = 2 \times 2 \times 2 \times 2 = 16$.

The number n is called the degree of the _____.

a. Rationalisation
c. Cubic function
b. Root
d. Difference of two squares

6. In linear algebra, a _____ matrix is a square matrix A whose transpose is also its negative; that is, it satisfies the equation:

$$A^T = -A$$

or in component form, if $A = (a_{ij})$:

$$a_{ij} = -a_{ji} \text{ for all i and j.}$$

108 Chapter 10. Complex Vectors and Matrices

For example, the following matrix is _____:

$$\begin{bmatrix} 0 & 2 & -1 \\ -2 & 0 & -4 \\ 1 & 4 & 0 \end{bmatrix}.$$

Compare this with a symmetric matrix whose transpose is the same as the matrix

$$A^T = A,$$

or to an orthogonal matrix, the transpose of which is equal to its inverse:

$$A^T = A^{-1}.$$

Sums and scalar products of _____ matrices are again _____. Hence, the _____ matrices form a vector space. Its dimension is $\frac{n(n-1)}{2}$.

a. Skew-symmetric
c. Duplication matrix

b. Bisymmetric matrix
d. Complex Hadamard matrix

7. In mathematics, a _____ is a rectangular array of numbers. This way, matrices can record data that depend on multiple parameters. In particular they are used to keep track of the coefficients of multiple linear equations. Matrices are closely connected to linear transformations, which are higher-dimensional analogs of linear functions, i.e., functions of the form f(x) = c Â· x, where c is a constant. This map corresponds to a _____ with one row and column, with entry c. In addition to a number of elementary, entrywise operations such as _____ addition a key notion is _____ multiplication, which displays a number of features not encountered in numbers; for example, products of matrices depend on the order of the factors, unlike products of real numbers, say, where c Â· d = d Â· c for any two numbers c and d.

a. Commutativity
c. Matrix

b. Heap
d. Polynomial expression

8. In mathematics, the _____, Hermitian transpose, or adjoint matrix of an m-by-n matrix A with complex entries is the n-by-m matrix A* obtained from A by taking the transpose and then taking the complex conjugate of each entry. The _____ is formally defined by

$$(A^*)_{ij} = \overline{A_{ji}}$$

where the subscripts denote the i,j-th entry, for 1 ≤ i ≤ n and 1 ≤ j ≤ m, and the overbar denotes a scalar complex conjugate. (The complex conjugate of a + bi, where a and b are reals, is a − bi.)

a. Complex conjugate
c. Change of basis
b. Conjugate transpose
d. Dual spaces

9. In abstract algebra, the _____ of a module is a measure of the module's 'size'. It is defined as the _____ of the longest ascending chain of submodules and is a generalization of the concept of dimension for vector spaces. The modules with finite _____ share many important properties with finite-dimensional vector spaces.
   a. Length
   c. Morita equivalence
   b. Finitely generated module
   d. Supermodule

10. In linear algebra, the _____ of a matrix A is another matrix A^T (also written A', A^{tr} or ^tA) created by any one of the following equivalent actions:

- write the rows of A as the columns of A^T
- write the columns of A as the rows of A^T
- reflect A by its main diagonal (which starts from the top left) to obtain A^T

Formally, the _____ of an m × n matrix A with elements A_{ij} is the n × m matrix

$$A^T_{ij} = A_{ji} \text{ for } 1 \leq i \leq n, 1 \leq j \leq m.$$

The _____ of a scalar is the same scalar.

- $\begin{bmatrix} 1 & 2 \end{bmatrix}^T = \begin{bmatrix} 1 \\ 2 \end{bmatrix}$.

- $\begin{bmatrix} 1 & 2 \\ 3 & 4 \end{bmatrix}^T = \begin{bmatrix} 1 & 3 \\ 2 & 4 \end{bmatrix}$.

- $\begin{bmatrix} 1 & 2 \\ 3 & 4 \\ 5 & 6 \end{bmatrix}^T = \begin{bmatrix} 1 & 3 & 5 \\ 2 & 4 & 6 \end{bmatrix}$.

For matrices A, B and scalar c we have the following properties of _____:

1. $\left(\mathbf{A}^T\right)^T = \mathbf{A}$

    Taking the _____ is an involution (self inverse.)

- $(\mathbf{A} + \mathbf{B})^T = \mathbf{A}^T + \mathbf{B}^T$

The _____ respects addition.

- $(\mathbf{AB})^T = \mathbf{B}^T\mathbf{A}^T$

    Note that the order of the factors reverses. From this one can deduce that a square matrix A is invertible if and only if A^T is invertible, and in this case we have $(A^{-1})^T = (A^T)^{-1}$. It is relatively easy to extend this result to the general case of multiple matrices, where we find that $(ABC...XYZ)^T = Z^TY^TX^T...C^TB^TA^T$.

- $(c\mathbf{A})^T = c\mathbf{A}^T$

    The _____ of a scalar is the same scalar. Together with (2), this states that the _____ is a linear map from the space of m × n matrices to the space of all n × m matrices.

- $\det(\mathbf{A}^T) = \det(\mathbf{A})$

    The determinant of a square matrix is the same as that of its _____.

- The dot product of two column vectors a and b can be computed as

$$\mathbf{a} \cdot \mathbf{b} = \mathbf{a}^T\mathbf{b},$$

which is written as $a_i\, b^i$ in Einstein notation.
- If A has only real entries, then A^TA is a positive-semidefinite matrix.
- $(\mathbf{A}^T)^{-1} = (\mathbf{A}^{-1})^T$

    The _____ of an invertible matrix is also invertible, and its inverse is the _____ of the inverse of the original matrix.

- If A is a square matrix, then its eigenvalues are equal to the eigenvalues of its _____.

A square matrix whose _____ is equal to itself is called a symmetric matrix; that is, A is symmetric if

$$\mathbf{A}^T = \mathbf{A}.$$

A square matrix whose _____ is also its inverse is called an orthogonal matrix; that is, G is orthogonal if

$$\mathbf{GG}^T = \mathbf{G}^T\mathbf{G} = \mathbf{I}_n,$$ the identity matrix, i.e. $G^T = G^{-1}$.

A square matrix whose _____ is equal to its negative is called skew-symmetric matrix; that is, A is skew-symmetric if

$$\mathbf{A}^T = -\mathbf{A}.$$

The conjugate _____ of the complex matrix A, written as A*, is obtained by taking the _____ of A and the complex conjugate of each entry:

$$\mathbf{A}^* = (\overline{\mathbf{A}})^T = \overline{(\mathbf{A}^T)}.$$

If f: V→W is a linear map between vector spaces V and W with nondegenerate bilinear forms, we define the _____ of f to be the linear map $^t f$: W→V, determined by

$$B_V(v,\,^t f(w)) = B_W(f(v), w) \quad \forall\; v \in V, w \in W.$$

Here, B_V and B_W are the bilinear forms on V and W respectively. The matrix of the _____ of a map is the transposed matrix only if the bases are orthonormal with respect to their bilinear forms.

Over a complex vector space, one often works with sesquilinear forms instead of bilinear (conjugate-linear in one argument.)

a. Drazin inverse
c. Levinson recursion

b. Tridiagonal matrix
d. Transpose

11. A _____ is a square matrix with complex entries which is equal to its own conjugate transpose -- that is, the element in the ith row and jth column is equal to the complex conjugate of the element in the jth row and ith column, for all indices i and j:

$$a_{i,j} = \overline{a_{j,i}}.$$

If the conjugate transpose of a matrix A is denoted by $A^\dagger$, then the Hermitian property can be written concisely as

$$A = A^\dagger.$$

For example,

$$\begin{bmatrix} 3 & 2+i \\ 2-i & 1 \end{bmatrix}$$

is a _____.

The entries on the main diagonal (top left to bottom right) of any _____ are necessarily real. A matrix that has only real entries is Hermitian if and only if it is a symmetric matrix, i.e., if it is symmetric with respect to the main diagonal.

- a. Permutation matrix
- b. Levinson recursion
- c. Hermitian matrix
- d. Symplectic matrix

12. In mathematics, a _____ is an n by n complex matrix U satisfying the condition

$$U^*U = UU^* = I_n$$

where I_n is the identity matrix and U^* is the conjugate transpose (also called the Hermitian adjoint) of U. Note this condition says that a matrix U is unitary if and only if it has an inverse which is equal to its conjugate transpose U^*

$$U^{-1} = U^*$$

A _____ in which all entries are real is the same thing as an orthogonal matrix. Just as an orthogonal matrix G preserves the (real) inner product of two real vectors,

$$\langle Gx, Gy \rangle = \langle x, y \rangle$$

so also a _____ U satisfies

$$\langle Ux, Uy \rangle = \langle x, y \rangle$$

for all complex vectors x and y, where $\langle \cdot, \cdot \rangle$ stands now for the standard inner product on C^n. If U is an n by n matrix then the following are all equivalent conditions:

1. U is unitary
2. U^* is unitary
3. the columns of U form an orthonormal basis of C^n with respect to this inner product
4. the rows of U form an orthonormal basis of C^n with respect to this inner product
5. U is an isometry with respect to the norm from this inner product

It follows from the isometry property that all eigenvalues of a _____ are complex numbers of absolute value 1 (i.e., they lie on the unit circle centered at 0 in the complex plane.) The same is true for the determinant.

a. Unitary matrix
b. Integer matrix
c. Unistochastic matrix
d. Unimodular matrix

13. In linear algebra, a _____ is a special kind of Toeplitz matrix where each row vector is rotated one element to the right relative to the preceding row vector. In numerical analysis circulant matrices are important because they are diagonalized by a discrete Fourier transform, and hence linear equations that contain them may be quickly solved using a fast Fourier transform. They can be interpreted analytically as the integral kernel of a convolution operator on the cyclic group In cryptography, a _____ is used in the MixColumns step of the Advanced Encryption Standard.

a. Pentadiagonal matrix
b. Minimum degree algorithm
c. Hilbert matrix
d. Circulant matrix

14. In its simplest meaning in mathematics and logic, an _____ is an action or procedure which produces a new value from one or more input values. There are two common types of operations: unary and binary. Unary operations involve only one value, such as negation and trigonometric functions.

a. AKS primality test
b. ADE classification
c. Abelian P-root group
d. Operation

15. The notion _____ is used in different, but similar ways:

A permutation P over a set S with k elements is called a _____ with offset t if and only if

the elements of S may be ordered (c < c < ... < c[k]) and the mapping of P may be written as:

p(c[i]) = c[i + t] for i = 1, 2, ..., k − t, and

p(c[i]) = c[i + t − k] for i = k − t + 1, k − t + 2, ..., k.

Note: Every _____ of definition type 1 will be constructed with exactly gcd (k, t) disjoint cycles; see cycles and fixed points.

a. Cycle graph
b. Linear span
c. Cyclic permutation
d. Near-ring

16. In several fields of mathematics the term _____ is used with different but closely related meanings. They all relate to the notion of mapping the elements of a set to other elements of the same set, i.e., exchanging (or 'permuting') elements of a set.

The general concept of _____ can be defined more formally in different contexts:

In combinatorics, a _____ is usually understood to be a sequence containing each element from a finite set once, and only once.

a. Binary function
b. Near-field
c. Permutation
d. Rupture field

ANSWER KEY

Chapter 1
1. d 2. d 3. b 4. b 5. a 6. a 7. d 8. d 9. c 10. d
11. d 12. a 13. b 14. b 15. c 16. c 17. b 18. b 19. a 20. d
21. d 22. d 23. c 24. a 25. d 26. d 27. d 28. c 29. a

Chapter 2
1. c 2. d 3. c 4. d 5. d 6. c 7. a 8. a 9. d 10. b
11. d 12. c 13. a 14. a 15. d 16. d 17. c 18. c 19. d 20. b
21. b 22. d 23. d 24. d 25. c 26. b 27. b 28. d 29. d 30. b
31. c 32. d 33. b 34. d 35. b 36. d 37. c 38. c 39. d 40. c
41. c 42. b 43. d 44. a 45. d 46. d 47. d 48. b 49. d 50. d
51. d 52. a 53. d 54. b

Chapter 3
1. d 2. d 3. d 4. b 5. a 6. d 7. a 8. d 9. d 10. a
11. d 12. c 13. c 14. a 15. d 16. d 17. d 18. b 19. d 20. d
21. d 22. d 23. b 24. b 25. a

Chapter 4
1. d 2. a 3. b 4. d 5. d 6. d 7. a 8. d 9. a 10. c
11. b 12. a 13. d 14. d 15. c 16. c 17. c 18. d 19. d 20. c
21. a 22. d 23. b 24. b 25. b 26. a 27. d 28. b 29. b 30. c
31. c 32. d 33. d

Chapter 5
1. b 2. d 3. d 4. d 5. c 6. c 7. b 8. d 9. a 10. c
11. b 12. d 13. c 14. c 15. a 16. b 17. d 18. a 19. d 20. d
21. d 22. c 23. c 24. d 25. a 26. a 27. d 28. d 29. d 30. a
31. d 32. b

Chapter 6
1. d 2. d 3. c 4. d 5. d 6. c 7. a 8. c 9. c 10. c
11. c 12. d 13. a 14. b 15. d 16. c 17. d 18. d 19. a 20. a
21. d 22. c 23. a 24. d 25. b 26. c 27. d 28. d 29. a 30. d
31. a 32. d 33. d 34. b 35. a 36. d 37. a 38. b 39. d 40. d
41. d 42. d 43. d 44. b 45. a 46. d 47. b 48. d 49. c 50. c
51. b 52. d 53. a 54. b 55. a 56. d 57. d 58. b 59. d 60. d
61. d 62. a 63. b 64. d 65. d 66. a 67. d 68. d 69. d 70. b

Chapter 7
1. c 2. c 3. d 4. d 5. d 6. c 7. c 8. d 9. d 10. d
11. d 12. d 13. c 14. c 15. c 16. d 17. d 18. b 19. d 20. d
21. d 22. d 23. d 24. d 25. b 26. b 27. a 28. b 29. d 30. d
31. d 32. a 33. c 34. c

Chapter 8
1. d	2. a	3. b	4. c	5. c	6. a	7. b	8. d	9. a	10. d
11. b	12. a	13. b	14. d	15. a	16. a	17. d	18. c	19. d	20. d
21. d	22. d	23. a	24. a	25. d	26. b	27. b	28. c	29. d	30. c

Chapter 9
1. c	2. d	3. b	4. d	5. b	6. c	7. c	8. d	9. d	10. b
11. d	12. c	13. c	14. d	15. d	16. d	17. d	18. d	19. b	20. b
21. a	22. c	23. d	24. d	25. d	26. a	27. b	28. d	29. a	30. d
31. d									

Chapter 10
1. b	2. a	3. d	4. c	5. b	6. a	7. c	8. b	9. a	10. d
11. c	12. a	13. d	14. d	15. c	16. c				

www.ingramcontent.com/pod-product-compliance
Lightning Source LLC
Chambersburg PA
CBHW082050230426
43670CB00016B/2843